PRESERVING
THE ITALIAN WAY

This book is dedicated to my parents,
Giuseppe and Domenica Demaio, for their
courage and wisdom, and for giving me
the opportunity to be who and what I am.

This book also proudly and lovingly
acknowledges the unfailing support of my
wife, Lynn, for her companionship in following
my every dream, and for embracing a mixed
bag of cultures, values and experiences with
enthusiasm and genuine pride.

Also, to my sons, Giuseppe, Carlo and
Alessandro, for their taking up the passion for
our shared heritage that has been handed to
me, and to my long-suffering friends, who
have put up with my questions, plans and
general ranting over a lifetime, as I worked
my way towards the realisation of this book.

PRESERVING
THE ITALIAN WAY

A collection of traditional
Italian *casalinga* recipes

Pietro Demaio

plum. Pan Macmillan Australia

Preface

Since I first self-published this collection of traditional Italian preserving recipes in 2008, I have been on an emotional journey of connecting with at least 45,000 readers. I have had hundreds of emails from fellow first-generation immigrant Italians and non-Italians alike, who have enjoyed becoming part of this food journey. I hope this updated edition finds a new and equally passionate audience.

Sharing and embracing our stories and histories is essential if we are to value who we are and who has come before us. This book is simply trying to keep alive one aspect of my Italian heritage. I hope that once you are on this journey, you will continue to enrich, explore and find connections within your culture and the world around you.

Bocca al lupo (good luck)!

Pietro

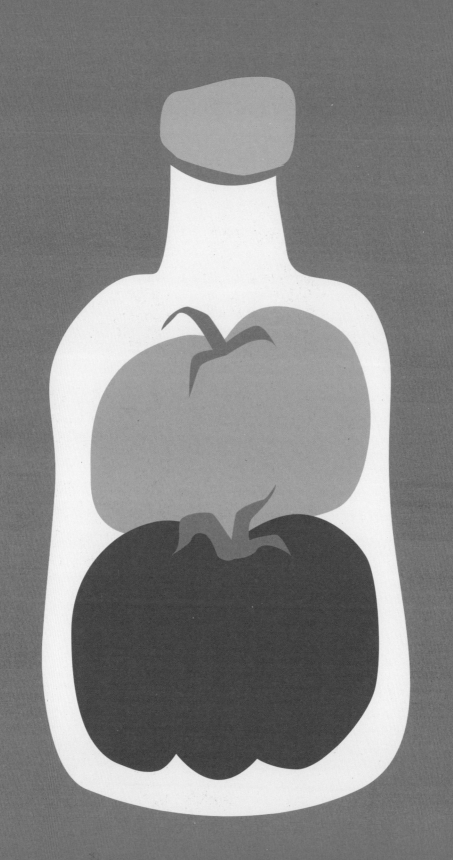

Contents

Introduction

Introduzione

My wife and I have a small farm on the Mornington Peninsula in Victoria, a few hours out of Melbourne, where we grow a few *zibibbo* vines, a Southern Italian grape variety. Each day, I have a cup of coffee at the local deli near my GP surgery, and over the years I have come to know the owners Frank and Gina, and Gina's sister Maria, quite well. I remember taking in some of my grapes for Maria one day, and on eating the very first one she began to cry. You can imagine my shock. What had I done wrong?

On the contrary, Maria, who was 75 at the time, told me that the instant she tasted the grape, she was immediately taken back to when she was four years old and her father would give her the first of the *zibibbo* grapes they grew on their own property in the Molise region of Italy. Maria had not eaten this variety since, and tasting them again reminded her of her father's kindness and pride. The *zibibbo* grapes are tasty, sweet and floral … but they have pips, so you won't find this variety in the supermarkets! This encounter reminded me of the power of food, the impact that it has on us, and its ability to stir up our deepest, most essential memories.

How often have you tasted something and been reminded of your grandmother, mother, a special friend, or of a visit to your home town? How many of our memories of special occasions revolve around food? For me, these memories are part of who we are. We sometimes don't realise that just under the surface of our memory is a whole lifetime of experiences, pleasures and events in our lives that influence every action we take.

As an Italian, certain foods that are special to an era or place hold huge significance; one that goes beyond heritage or genetics or cultural identity. The closest comparison I can make is with the Indigenous Australian concept of The Dreaming – that mystical connection between who we are and where we have come from, and what we hold precious and essential to our identity. But I fear that with the passage of time and another generation, irreplaceable links with our culture will be lost; not only here in Australia but even at 'home' in Italy where, because of the progress in rural villages, nobody prepares food as our mothers did. The evenings sitting around the table, tasting a fine cheese or a crusty piece of bread with a tangy, salty sardine and a glass of homemade wine, will vanish into memories, and with them a bond that ties all Italians together will be lost forever.

How can I ever thank my parents for having the courage and vision to leave this place, which was their home? They set out for a distant land, totally illiterate and without any resources other than their love for one another and their family. The hope was that there would be an opportunity to make a better life: no guarantees, no social security, no falling back.

My father, like many others, came to Australia in 1937. He left a pregnant wife behind in Italy, as well as four children ranging from three to eight years of age. They were not to see one another for a further 10 years. For half that time, thanks to the war, they couldn't even send letters to reassure one another that they were safe.

In 1948, they were reunited and continued their total dedication and commitment to better the life and opportunities of their family. This is the true Italian culture.

When I returned to their village of Varapodio, in the province of Reggio Calabria in Southern Italy – 'l'umbilico della civilizazione' (the umbilicus of civilisation) – in 1986, I was moved to tears when I was told by their contemporaries of the goodness, kindness and fairness of my father, and the dedication and hard work of my mother. I remember my first day there, walking into a cafe and ordering an espresso. I did not introduce myself, but being a small village, everyone knew that I was the 'Americano'. After I had my coffee, I went to pay. The barista said that the coffee was on the house. How could this be? He replied that he remembered the many pieces of bread that my mother had given to him as a child during the war, 70 years before! I hope that I might have such an impact on someone someday.

Even though I truly love Australia, I still have a passion for and a connection to the land of my forefathers. Whenever I go back to Varapodio, I vividly recall the hundreds of stories that I have heard over and over again from my grandmother and my parents. They talked about a time when there was a different level of respect for each other, and in particular for the *compare*[1]; or the feast of San Giovanni; or when an entire village would set out merrily on foot to attend a festa della Madonna (feast of the Virgin), a two to three day walk away. Every step through the village, every corner, every clump of cane or rocky riverbed is full of history and the tales that my parents told me. This is a part of me to which I will always go back, even if only in spirit.

Every time I return to Italy, I am amazed at how food is a medium for familiarity with people I barely know. We are able to share the same passion for the *rosamarina* (see page 160) in Calabria, savour a good pecorino cheese in Toscana, sip *limoncino* liqueur together in Ischia (see page 243), or enjoy a great slice of speck in Treviso or Pordenone. Food is the common language. How wonderful it is to share that language and sample new experiences and tastes with others. Even more exciting, my children now equate being Italian with that intense, patient and generous hospitality that is so unique to Italy; that rich ambience that is found even in the poorest villages.

When my children are asked, 'What are you?' they respond, 'I am Italian but I am an Australian.' They carry their heritage with pride, not as a burden. They understand and respect the heart-breaking choice my parents had to make to leave their home and settle in a faraway land. At the same time, my children understand that Italy was not a place to flee but that there are, and were, many wonderful people and places that were left behind in the search of a better life.

I want to give something to my children. I think that a love for the food and, in particular, the traditions that are handed down from parents to their children need to be recorded. The recipe for a particular preserve or salami will maintain our links with a very courageous and inspired generation that left their homeland to give us, their children and grandchildren, the opportunity to live in a land of equality, justice, relative safety and where anything is still possible for anyone who wants to take on a challenge.

My passion has been to collect as many of the traditional, often ancient and sometimes forgotten recipes, and also the day-to-day dishes that are typical of a region. That way, we can share them with our friends, and hand them on to our children as a legacy of our background. To involve our next generation.

As has happened so often in recent times, older traditional methods of food preparation that produced a wide range of aromatic, flavoursome and regionally typical products, have given way to the standardised, poor-quality, bland, soulless products that appear on our supermarket shelves. They need to be cheap to produce and must appeal to the widest range of customers. The 'slow food' movement has been passionate about identifying, documenting and promoting traditional quality primary products. These foods are produced regionally with locally sourced ingredients using traditional methods. I suppose this book is about trying to document and demystify those methods.

The origin of many Italian preserves is from a time long before refrigerators and supermarkets, when a family's larder needed to be stocked with food for winter. At their disposal were the local seasonal produce, salt, olive oil and the sun. Over the years, a number of delicious methods were developed to maintain the nutritional value as well as enhance the flavour of a number of different foods as they became abundant. Each region, and each family within that region, developed slight variations that made their particular method special and a real source of pride for that family.

When I was researching recipes for this book, I was often directed to an aunt or a cousin who did a particular preserve or salami in a specific and often 'secret' way. Often, the recipes were a basic standard, with variations that were particular to a family or region, each family then claiming that their variation was the only authentic or best way to make a certain dish. All these variations are a part of the fabric that connects us, yet they also help us find our unique way of expressing ourselves.

When a friend serves us a slice of salami they've made, or a sample of a preserve they've prepared in the traditional way, it is very special. It opens up a whole conversation where we speak with pride of our families and their memories, and debate the delicate but specific beauty of the tastes that are only achieved when food is prepared in this way.

This discussion is the healthy rivalry and ownership of our heritage, and the unique quality of modern Italy – rich and diverse ancient backgrounds with a mingling of numerous cultures and people over millennia, each making up part of our genetic and cultural identity. This, to me, is worth preserving in as many ways as possible, and food is always, and always will be, the central feature bonding our culture together. If we lose this, we will lose the most essential ingredient of our identity.

Of course, when it came to asking my relatives and other people for their traditional recipes that have been passed down, the instructions were typically

Italian – in other words, 'a little of this' or 'a good measure of that' or 'whatever you like'! So it has taken a bit of trial and error to get these recipes just right so you can feel confident trying them yourself at home, but do remember that *instinct* is also a key Italian ingredient!

With the incredible vegetables and fresh ingredients we have in Australia, combined with the traditional Italian methods of preserving, I'm sure you'll have great success and joy with these recipes. I hope they grace your table often and connect you to a previous generation of very brave and selfless loved ones.

Pietro

---

1   *Compare* is the word used for godfather, or the best man at your wedding, or someone who is chosen to be a very special associate, adviser and companion. In Southern Italy, a *compare* (or *commare*, for a woman) is respected and often held in higher esteem than a relative. You can choose your friends, but you can't choose your relatives, as the saying goes!

Preserving notes

There are many different ways that food can be preserved, as you will see, but there are a few essentials to bear in mind:

* Use a good-quality extra-virgin olive oil. Olive oil is the backbone of many of the recipes in this book and using a decent one will make all the difference.
* Use the best and freshest ingredients that are available to you. If you are able to grow some vegetables and herbs yourself, do! It takes the same amount of work to use good-quality products as to use poor-quality ones, but the results are totally different.
* Think seasonally. Make sure that the ingredients you are preserving are at peak season. Don't try to make tomato sauce during the winter, for example.
* Ensure that you follow the sterilisation instructions as closely as possible (see page 21).

Also, remember that many of these recipes were originally developed at a time when there were no commutes, no trains to catch, no need to ferry children to or from school or birthday parties. There are more demands on our time now in the modern world and I understand the desire to keep things simple and quick.

But this kind of cooking takes patience and time. So make sure you have plenty of both and invite friends around to help. A large part of the pleasure and success of preserving the Italian way is to spend time with your friends, your *compare* or *commare*, your relatives and your children, building a bank of memories together, creating food to share. That is the Italian way.

Most common preserving techniques

The four main ways to preserve food are as follows:

Preserving in oil

Conserve sott'olio

The vegetables are cooked or cured first, then mixed with the desired flavourings. Finally, the vegetables are covered in extra-virgin olive oil and sealed in jars. See pages 23–47 for more information.

Preserving in vinegar

Conserve sott'aceto

The vegetables are cooked or cured first, then placed in jars. A mixture of vinegar, water and spices is brought to the boil, then poured over the vegetables while still hot (thus ensuring the vinegar is sterile). The lids are immediately put on the jars so that they seal hermetically as the vinegar mixture cools. See pages 49–61 for more information.

Preserving in brine

Conserve in salamoia

The vegetables are cooked or cured first, then transferred to a brine (water and salt) solution and kept submerged in the brine using a weight for a period of time. When ready, the vegetables usually need to be rinsed or transferred to a fresh (not salted) water solution. You will find recipes using this technique throughout this book.

Preserving in salt

Conserve sotto sale

The vegetables or seafood/meat are mixed with a large quantity of salt and left at room temperature for the specified amount of time, with any brine that forms drained and discarded. When ready, the vegetables or seafood/ meat are layered with more salt – finishing with a thick layer of salt on top to cover – and either transferred to jars or kept in a large container submerged under a weight to continue to cure. You will find recipes using this technique throughout this book.

A note on sterilisation

Proper sterilisation is an essential process that needs to be followed meticulously. Poorly sterilised food will ferment and explode or, worse still, can be poisonous and extremely dangerous. The basic process for hermetically sealing produce using a hot water bath technique is as follows:

1   Choose clean, unchipped glass jars with matching metal lids. Ensure that the lids are clean and their rubber seals are intact. If there is any visible corrosion or damage to the seal, do not use the lid.

2   Clean the jars and lids by running them through a hot cycle in the dishwasher or by washing them in hot, soapy water.

3   Pack your chosen produce into the jars. It is important to pack fairly tightly, as the produce can shift and settle during the sterilisation process.

4   Cover the produce with brine, vinegar or oil, ensuring that it is completely covered by at least 1 cm. Always leave an approximately 2 cm gap at the top of your jars before sealing (if the jars are overfilled, they will explode during the sterilising process). Wipe the rims of the jars well to ensure that the seal is as tight as it can be. Screw on the lids.

5   Place a clean towel in the bottom of a large stockpot and sit your jars of produce on top. Fill the pot with water to 1 cm below the brim of the shortest jar and cover with a lid to maintain the temperature.

6   *Slowly* bring the water to the desired temperature of 80–100°C to ensure that the jars and their contents are heated evenly. This will take around 40 minutes. Once the water reaches the desired temperature – i.e. simmering to just-boiling point – maintain the temperature for the time specified in the recipe. Note that different produce will require different simmering times, such as at least 20 minutes for fruit, 1 hour for tomatoes or 2 hours for tuna.

7   Turn off the heat and allow the jars to cool in the water. After 36 hours, check the lids to ensure they have remained sealed; the centre of the lid should be firm and drawn inwards. If the lid has popped out it has *not* sealed, so you will need to use the produce immediately or repeat the above process using a different lid. I find I can use lids two or three times before having to change them, though sometimes only twice if they've been used for acidic or salty preserves.

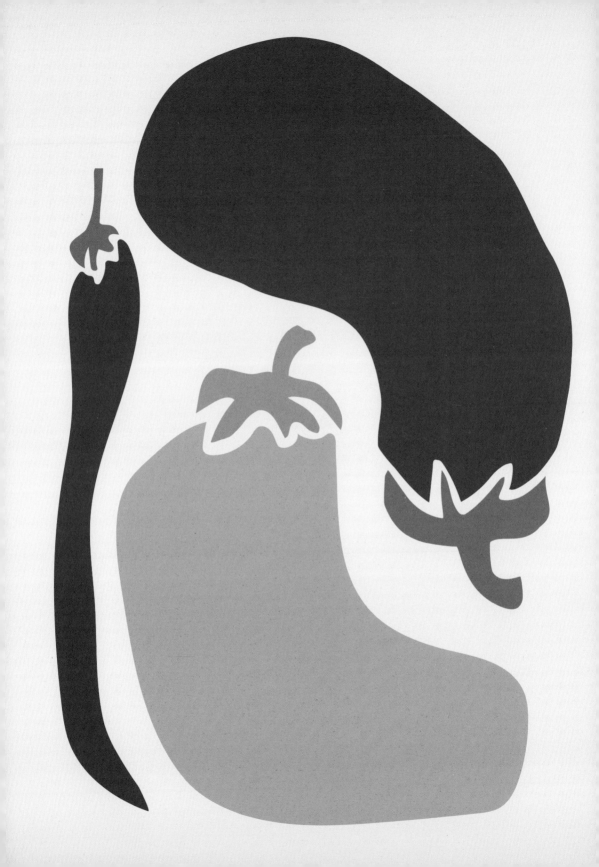

VEGETABLES IN OIL

CONSERVE SOTT'OLIO

01

Sott'olio (under oil) is a common and versatile method used to preserve almost any vegetable. There are basically two parts to the process. The first part is cooking, which can be done with heat or with salt and vinegar (which essentially cooks the vegetables by producing a chemical reaction). The second part is sealing the preserved products from air and bacteria, either under oil or by sealing hermetically in a hot water bath (see page 21).

Almost all vegetables can be preserved but they need to be very fresh and clean. Different vegetables are often mixed together for their appearance rather than taste – such as _peperoni rossi_ (red capsicum) with _melanzane_ (eggplant) or _pomodori verdi_ (green tomatoes) with _carote_ (carrots). This achieves a variation in texture as well as colour. You will notice that the patriotic trilogy of white, red and green representing the national flag is a common feature in Italian food!

The basic technique described below can be used with most vegetables:

1 Prepare the vegetables you're going to use and then place slices/strips in layers in a plastic tub. Liberally sprinkle salt over each layer and repeat until you've used all the vegetables.

2 Position a plate or wooden tray on top of the salted vegetables and place a 10 kg weight (about four bricks is ideal) on top. Leave the vegetables for 24 hours.

3 Drain off any liquid and loosen the vegetables with your hands.

4 Add the quantity of vinegar specified in the recipe (usually 500 ml) and mix thoroughly, then set aside for 1 hour. Replace the plate or tray and weight and leave for a further 12 hours.

5 Drain the vegetables and squeeze out any excess liquid with your hands. Transfer to a large bowl and add the extra flavouring ingredients as specified in the recipe.

6 Layer the vegetables with extra-virgin olive oil in jars, topping up with a final layer of olive oil to completely cover. This is what 'seals' the preserve, so to speak. As long as the vegetables stay under the oil they will be safe to eat. Or you can seal your preserve following the sterilising instructions on page 21. _Semplice_!

'When I went to Catholic school in Melbourne as a child in the 1960s, my mother would make my lunch: two thick slabs of homemade bread with a generous loading of *melanzane* and *peperoni sott'olio*. As I ate, the air around me would reek of garlic and the oil would drip down my arm to my elbow. All of my friends, who had Vegemite or jam sandwiches, wouldn't come near me. I was literally a social outcast.

When my son went to a public school in the 1990s, I used to send him off with a salad dressed in oil and vinegar, some *sott'olio* and crusty bread. All the other children would beg him for a taste of this interesting food because their Vegemite or jam sandwiches were so boring!

Moral of the story: you might feel you are weird or an outcast, but just wait a while and you will be the centre of attention.'

Vegetables in Oil

Eggplants

Eggplants in oil

Melanzane sott'olio

For this recipe, look for deep-purple eggplants that are large and firm with a shiny, taut skin. Inside there should not be many seeds.

6 large eggplants, peeled and cut lengthways into
    3–4 mm thick slices, then into 5 mm wide strips
500 g table salt
500 ml white wine vinegar
60 g dried oregano
2 teaspoons dried chilli flakes
5–6 garlic cloves, roughly chopped
extra-virgin olive oil, to cover

Special equipment
plastic tub
10 kg weight (about 4 bricks is ideal)

Place a layer of eggplant in the bottom of the plastic tub. Liberally sprinkle salt over the top and continue layering until you've used all the eggplant and salt.

Position a plate or wooden tray on top of the salted eggplant and place a 10 kg weight on top. Leave the eggplant strips for 24 hours, after which time they will have produced a dark, salty liquid. Remove the weights, drain and discard the liquid and loosen the slightly dry eggplant strips with your hands.

Pour over the vinegar and mix thoroughly, then set aside for 1 hour (the eggplant will absorb the vinegar). Replace the plate or tray and weight and leave for a further 12 hours.

Drain the eggplant strips and squeeze out any excess liquid with your hands. Transfer the eggplant to a large bowl and mix through the dried oregano, chilli flakes and garlic.

Pour a splash of olive oil into a clean jar (see steps 1–2, page 21) and top with a layer of the eggplant mixture, pressing down to remove any air bubbles. Continue to fill the jar with the eggplant mixture, adding a drizzle of oil between each layer to ensure that the oil is evenly distributed throughout the jar. Finally, press firmly on the eggplant and cover with a final drizzle of olive oil, ensuring that the eggplant is completely submerged in the oil. Repeat with as many jars as you need.

Check the eggplant after 2–3 days and, if necessary, top up with oil as the eggplant will have soaked up some of the liquid.

Seal the jars and store in a cool, dark place for 3 months, after which time the eggplant will still be sharp and crunchy. It will keep for up to 1 year but it will not be at its peak. Once opened, store the eggplant in the fridge, where it will keep for up to 1 month.

Tip: There are almost limitless variations to this recipe, depending on what is in season. These include mixing the eggplant with any or all of the following ingredients: green tomatoes, green or red capsicums, zucchini, celery, carrots, green beans, chokos or onions. The extra vegetables are sliced and mixed with the eggplant at the beginning and are therefore salted and pickled in the same way.

Variation

Signora Francesca's layered eggplants
Fette di melanzane della Signora Francesca

Follow the recipe as above but instead of adding the oregano, chilli and garlic before layering in the jars, keep those ingredients separate and add a little at a time between the layers of eggplant, together with 30–40 dried basil leaves (or use Salted Basil, see page 103) and 500 g sun-dried tomatoes. A bit like a lasagne – a layer of eggplant, then garlic, then dried oregano, dried basil, sun-dried tomatoes and finally a sprinkle of chilli flakes, then cover with more eggplant and repeat. When all the eggplant is used up, press firmly and cover with a final layer of olive oil to ensure the eggplant is completely submerged.

'Ischia is an island in the Bay of Naples where my dear friends, the Strina family, live. Antonio runs a plant nursery and is the creator of the famous garden La Mortilla. It is the home of the late Sir William Walton. He settled there in the 1930s with his Argentinian ballerina wife, Lady Susan Walton, and created a haven for the study of music. I visited her and the garden one day with Antonio. Ebullient, intelligent and totally dedicated, Lady Susan proudly took me around the garden overlooking the Bay of Naples with a magenta sunset. That night, I called my wife to tell her of my inspiring day and she told me that Sir William Walton was her mother's second cousin! It is such a small world.

The island of Ischia is a jewel of history, with rugged beauty and amazing food exploding with flavours nurtured by the Neapolitan sun. It is a volcanic island that is literally bursting with natural hot springs and jets of hot sulphurous air. Even food is buried and cooked by the volcanic energy in its pits! We visited there with our children in the summer of 1986. This was their first trip to Italy and they found it hard to believe that they would not wake up and find themselves in a dark bedroom, back in Melbourne in the middle of winter.'

Signora Francesca's Ischitana recipe for baby eggplants

Ricetta Ischitana della Signora Francesca per le melanzane

This recipe is a delicious way to use smaller eggplants, sometimes referred to as Lebanese eggplants, that are slender (like a zucchini) with quite a thin skin, hence no need to peel. They have a sweet, delicate flavour that is accentuated by the punchy, sharp flavours of capers and olives. You can also add a slice of hot chilli to each eggplant half if you like (or dare!). Jars of capers and olives are common pantry items in Italian homes and, in recipes such as these, you would use these from your store of dried olives or a jar you already had open or lying around. In an attempt to be precise, I would suggest you buy yourself some lovely dried black olives and a jar of capers and whatever you don't use for this recipe, I'm sure you'll be able to use in many other ways – like the other eggplant recipes in this book!

1 kg small (Lebanese) eggplants
500 g table salt
500 ml white wine vinegar
dried pitted black olives (1 per eggplant)
capers (2–3 per eggplant)
4 tablespoons dried oregano, or to taste
3 garlic cloves, finely sliced, or to taste
dried bay leaves (optional)
extra-virgin olive oil, to cover

Special equipment
plastic tub
10 kg weight (about 4 bricks is ideal)

Cut the eggplants in half but leave them connected at the stem (so don't cut them completely in half). Place them gently in the plastic tub and cover with the table salt.

Position a plate or wooden tray on top of the eggplant and place a 10 kg weight on top. Leave for 12 hours.

Remove the weights, then drain the eggplant, discard the liquid and cover with the white wine vinegar. Mix well, then replace the plate or tray and weight and leave for a further 12 hours.

Drain the eggplant and allow to dry slightly.

Between each pair of eggplant halves, place a dried black olive, two or three capers, a sprinkling of oregano and a slice of garlic. Press the two halves together and place them in clean jars (see steps 1–2, page 21). Add more sliced garlic, oregano or bay leaves to the jars, if desired, then completely cover in oil and seal.

Store in a cool, dark place for 1 month before eating. The eggplant will keep for up to 1 year unopened. Once opened, store in the fridge, where it will keep for up to 1 month. Enjoy with crusty bread.

Eggplant recipe from Ciccio's mother

Ricetta di melanzane della mamma di Ciccio

Enjoy these with a nice glass of Chianti or a homemade red and you will be in heaven!

6 large eggplants, peeled and cut lengthways into 2 mm thick slices
500 g table salt
500 ml white wine vinegar
30 anchovy fillets in oil, drained and halved lengthways
1–2 tablespoons capers (preferably in vinegar)
3 garlic cloves, finely sliced
5 long red chillies, finely sliced
1 tablespoon dried oregano
extra-virgin olive oil, to cover

Special equipment
plastic tub
10 kg weight (about 4 bricks is ideal)

Place a layer of eggplant in the bottom of the plastic tub. Liberally sprinkle salt over the top and continue layering until you've used all the eggplant and salt.

Position a plate or wooden tray on top of the eggplant and place a 10 kg weight on top. Leave the eggplant slices for 24 hours, after which time they will have produced a dark, salty liquid. Remove the weights, drain and discard the liquid, then loosen the slightly dry eggplant slices with your hands.

Pour over the white wine vinegar and mix thoroughly, then set aside for 1 hour (the eggplant will absorb the vinegar). Replace the plate or tray and weight and leave for a further 12 hours.

Drain the eggplant slices and squeeze out any excess liquid with your hands.

Lay the eggplant slices on a clean work surface and place half an anchovy fillet, a caper, a sliver of garlic and a slice of chilli on each slice, then roll the eggplant around the stuffing to make small parcels.

Arrange the eggplant parcels in clean jars (see steps 1–2, page 21), packing them fairly tightly. Sprinkle in the oregano, then cover with oil, ensuring the eggplant is completely submerged. Seal.

Store in a cool, dark place for 1 month before eating. The eggplant will keep for up to 1 year unopened. Once opened, store in the fridge, where it will keep for up to 1 month.

Rosa's fried eggplant preserve

Melanzane l'iscapeci di Rosa

6 large eggplants, cut lengthways into 5 mm
    thick slices
table salt
extra-virgin olive oil, for pan-frying and to cover
4 garlic cloves, finely sliced
splash of white wine vinegar
1 tablespoon dried mint

Spread the eggplant slices over one or more large trays, sprinkle liberally with salt and allow to stand for 1 hour.

Drain off any liquid and rinse off the excess salt. Pat dry.

Fry the eggplant slices (you'll have to do this in batches) in a splash of olive oil until lightly brown on both sides. Place on a tray and add the garlic, another splash of olive oil, the white wine vinegar and mint. Mix well.

Following the instructions on page 21, place the mixture in clean jars and completely cover with oil, leaving a 2 cm gap at the top of the jars. Screw on the lids and seal the jars hermetically in a hot water bath for 20 minutes to ensure they are airtight.

Store in a cool, dark place for 1 month before eating. The eggplant will keep for up to 1 year unopened. Once opened, store in the fridge, where it will keep for up to 1 month.

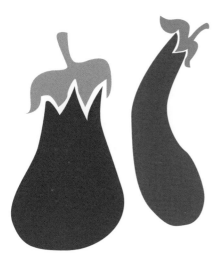

Halved baby eggplants in oil with chilli and mint

Meta' melanzane sott'olio con peperoncino e menta

As with Signora Francesca's Ischitana Recipe for Baby Eggplants (see page 31), this preserve is ideal for using the smaller, more delicate eggplants known as Lebanese eggplants. When ready, these can be eaten as is with crusty bread, as part of an antipasto spread, or even tossed through some pasta.

1 kg small (Lebanese) eggplants, sliced in half
    lengthways, stem removed
500 g table salt
2 garlic cloves, finely sliced
1 teaspoon dried chilli flakes
1 teaspoon dried mint
extra-virgin olive oil, to cover

Special equipment
plastic tub
10 kg weight (about 4 bricks is ideal)

Place the halved eggplants in the plastic tub and cover liberally with the table salt.

Position a plate or wooden tray on top of the eggplant and place a 10 kg weight on top. Leave for 24 hours.

Remove the weights, then drain the eggplant and discard the liquid. Rinse off the excess salt and squeeze the eggplant halves dry with your hands.

Mix the eggplant halves with the garlic, chilli flakes and mint, then place in clean jars (see steps 1–2, page 21). Cover with oil, then either mix with a spoon or place a lid on the jar and shake to ensure that the oil is thoroughly combined with the eggplant mixture. Add more oil to cover, ensuring the eggplant is completely submerged. Seal.

Store in a cool, dark place for 1 month before eating. The eggplant will keep for up to 1 year unopened. Once opened, store in the fridge, where it will keep for up to 1 month.

Compare Frank's eggplants

Melanzane alla Compare Franco

In Italy, a *compare* is like a godfather; someone who is chosen to be a very special associate, adviser and companion. You are, of course, allowed to have more than one *compare*. Frank is just one of mine!

If you can't find wild fennel (it often grows along the side of the road – though that's not always the best place to pick it from due to pollutants from cars!), substitute 2 tablespoons of dried fennel seeds. Likewise, if finding whole dried chillies proves hard, substitute 2 tablespoons of chilli flakes. But I would encourage you to buy or make your own Dried Hot Chillies (see page 109) as it makes the chilli flavour more subtle. This preserve is wonderful as part of an antipasto spread.

table salt
4 kg large eggplants, cut lengthways into
    3–4 mm thick slices
5 garlic cloves, finely sliced
2 tablespoons dried oregano
15 basil leaves
large handful of mint leaves
2 tablespoons wild fennel (seeds and finely
    chopped stalks)
7 whole dried red chillies, finely chopped

Special equipment
small wooden or plastic discs the same size
    as the opening of the jars you are using

Bring a large stockpot of salted water to the boil, as if you were preparing to cook pasta.

Drop the eggplant gently into the pot; when the salty water comes to the boil again, remove the eggplant and drain.

Allow the eggplant to cool, then distribute evenly among clean jars (see steps 1–2, page 21), alternating layers with a sprinkle of salt, garlic, oregano, basil, mint, fennel and chilli.

After the last layer of eggplant, add a final sprinkling of salt and then a disc of plastic or wood to keep the preserve submerged. Cover with oil and seal. Repeat with the remaining jars.

Store in a cool, dark place for 1 month before eating. The eggplant will keep for up to 1 year unopened. Once opened, store in the fridge, where it will keep for up to 3 months.

Eggplants in vinegar and oil

Melanzane sott'aceto e olio

This might seem like a lot of salt for just three eggplants, but I promise you, when you eat them they are not salty. They also have a softer texture than the standard *melanzane sott'olio*. You have the option of eating these straight away or preserving them to eat later. Either way, they are wonderful eaten cold from the fridge or served with barbecued meat on a summer's day.

1 litre white wine vinegar
2 tablespoons table salt, plus 1 teaspoon extra
3 eggplants, cut into 2 cm cubes
extra-virgin olive oil
5 garlic cloves, finely sliced
3 teaspoons dried oregano
chilli powder (optional)

Combine the white wine vinegar and the 2 tablespoons of salt with 1 litre of water in a large stockpot and place over high heat. Bring the mixture to the boil.

Once boiling, carefully drop in the eggplant cubes and wait for the mixture to return to the boil. Set your timer and allow to cook for 1 minute only, otherwise the eggplant will become too soft. Take the pot off the heat and drain, letting the eggplant dry off.

Place a splash of olive oil in the bottom of a clean jar (see steps 1–2, page 21), then add enough eggplant cubes to almost fill. Repeat with as many jars as you need.

To each jar, add slivers of garlic, some oregano, extra salt and chilli powder (if using) to taste, then cover with oil, ensuring the eggplant is completely submerged but there is still a 2 cm gap at the top of the jars.

If you plan to eat the eggplant fresh, you do not need to hermetically seal the jars at this stage. Simply screw on the lids and store the jars in the fridge, where the eggplant will keep for up to 3 months.

If you want to keep the eggplant for longer, seal the jars hermetically (see page 21) in a hot water bath for 20 minutes to ensure they are airtight, then store in a cool, dark place for up to 6 months. Once opened, the eggplant will keep for up to 1 year in the fridge.

Explosive mixture

Caviar Calabrese

This recipe is for the Calabrese readers, or anyone who dares! It is best served on bruschetta or toasted bread with a glass of wine at the beginning of a meal.

On one of my too few trips to Italy to be with my dear friend Ciccio, I was truly flattered to find that he had kept a small jar of this mixture, which I had sent to him via post, under lock and key, to be portioned out only to very special people. As a gift to him for hosting me for a week, I made him 10 jars and it was as if I had given him a new lease on life! And maybe I had, for who knows what the medicinal effects of this explosive mixture may be?

That week I spent with him was filled with indulgences, including one evening when he served ricotta with stinging nettles, cooked snails, homemade speck, eight varieties of Sardinian pecorino, four varieties of grappa and his famous Amaro (and later, the most severe attack of indigestion).

When Ciccio opened his restaurant, I was lucky enough to be there to help. We served 18 kg of this mixture to more than 500 guests. Most of them, being Tuscan, were nervous to try something 'chilli hot', as they say. But with encouragement, almost everyone did. After a while, it was obvious that the guests who did not like 'chilli hot' were coming back for more!

2 large eggplants, cut into 5 mm thick rounds
2 small zucchini, cut into 5 mm thick rounds
2–3 red capsicums, cut lengthways into strips
500 g green tomatoes, sliced
10 small red chillies, cut lengthways into strips
    (or to taste, depending on how hot you like it)
300 g table salt
500 ml white wine vinegar
4 garlic cloves, finely sliced
1 teaspoon dried oregano
10 sun-dried tomatoes, cut into strips
20 pitted green olives in brine (or you can use
    green olives already marinated in chilli and
    garlic, known as *schiacciate*)
capers, marinated mushrooms or other
    preserved vegetables, to taste (optional)
about 500 ml extra-virgin olive oil

Special equipment
plastic tub
10 kg weight (about 4 bricks is ideal)
meat mincer (optional)

Place the eggplant, zucchini, capsicum, green tomato and chilli in the plastic tub and mix well with the salt. Position a plate or wooden tray over them, then place a 10 kg weight on top. Leave for 24 hours.

Remove the weights. Drain and discard any liquid from the vegetables, then add the white wine vinegar. Mix well and leave to stand for 30 minutes to allow the vinegar to be absorbed. Replace the plate or tray and weight and leave for a further 24 hours.

Drain off any liquid and place the mixture in a large, clean mixing bowl, adding the garlic, oregano, sun-dried tomato and olives, together with 3 tablespoons of the olive oil. Mix well. You could also add capers, marinated mushrooms or any other preserved vegetables you like at this stage.

Now it's time to make the explosion! Ideally, pass the mixture through a meat mincer, using the fine grind and four blades. You can also blend the mixture in a food processor or with a hand-held blender, but use the pulse function and don't blend it for too long or you will end up with a paste. The texture should be very coarse, like a chunky pesto or salsa.

Place a couple of tablespoons of olive oil in each clean jar (see steps 1–2, page 21) before you fill them, to ensure that the mixture has the oil mixed throughout. Distribute the mixture among the jars and then top with the remaining olive oil and seal.

Store in a cool, dark place and check after 2–3 days to ensure the oil level hasn't dropped too much. If it has, top it up. If the mixture comes into contact with air, it will turn a dark brown colour rather than maintain its multicoloured hues. It will still taste nice but looks are important too!

The mixture under oil will keep for up to 1 year unopened. Once opened, store in the fridge, where it will keep for up to 1 month.

Capsicums

Capsicums in oil
Peperoni sott'olio

10 green or red capsicums
   (roughly 1 kg), quartered
500 ml white wine vinegar
2 dried bay leaves
1 teaspoon sugar
table salt, to taste
5 garlic cloves, finely sliced
extra-virgin olive oil, to cover

Place the capsicum on a baking tray and leave to dry on a bench for 24 hours. Cut the dried quarters into strips roughly 3 cm wide.

Bring the white wine vinegar, bay leaves and sugar to the boil in a large stockpot. Add salt to taste, as if you were salting water to cook pasta.

Add the capsicum and cook for 1–2 minutes, then turn off the heat. Allow to cool for 30 minutes, then drain, discarding the vinegar mixture and bay leaves. Place the capsicum on a clean tea towel and allow to dry for 24 hours.

When ready, place the capsicum in clean jars (see steps 1–2, page 21), add the garlic and cover with oil, ensuring the capsicum is completely submerged. Seal.

Store in a cool, dark place for 1 month before eating. The capsicum will keep for up to 1 year unopened. Once opened, store in the fridge, where it will keep for up to 1 month.

Variation
Connie's capsicums in oil
Peperoni sott'olio di donna Concetta

Follow the recipe above but use a mixture of red and yellow capsicums already cut into 3 cm strips. Skip the initial drying and go straight to the cooking in vinegar. Instead of garlic, place a dried bay leaf in each jar.

Capsicum parcels
Involtini di peperoni

1 litre vinegar
table salt, to taste
2 dried bay leaves
4 large red and yellow capsicums, cut into
   3 cm strips
anchovy fillets in oil (1 per capsicum strip)
2–3 long red chillies, sliced
capers (1 per capsicum strip)
2 garlic cloves, finely sliced (optional)
extra-virgin olive oil, to cover

Combine the vinegar and 500 ml of water in a large stockpot and add salt to taste, as if you were preparing to cook pasta. Add the bay leaves and bring to the boil.

Once boiling, add the capsicum strips. Return to the boil, then cook for 2 minutes (set a timer – they will be too soft if they cook for any longer). Drain.

Take a capsicum strip, place an anchovy fillet, a slice of chilli and a caper in the middle of the strip and roll the capsicum around the filling. Secure with a toothpick and place in a clean jar (see steps 1–2, page 21). Repeat with the remaining capsicum strips and jars.

Once you have filled the jars with *involtini*, add some more bay leaves and slices of garlic, if desired, and completely cover with oil. Seal.

Store in a cool, dark place for 1 month before eating. The *involtini* will keep for up to 1 year unopened. Once opened, store in the fridge, where it will keep for up to 1 month.

Variation
Capsicums, Neapolitan style
Peperoni alla Napoletana

Follow the recipe above but replace the chilli and bay leaves with fresh basil and oregano leaves.

Artichokes

Globe artichokes in oil

Carciofi sott'olio

Artichokes look difficult to prepare, but once you remove all the dark outer leaves you'll expose the soft tender heart (a bit like us Italians!). Simply peel or cut away the dark outer leaves until you are left with pale green leaves that feel soft to the touch. Cut off the stem and the top third of the leaves, exposing the heart, then use a teaspoon to gently scrape out the hairy 'choke' that circles the heart.

These artichokes in oil are excellent quartered and used in a salad or as part of an antipasto platter. Buy the small artichokes, about 3 cm in diameter, at the beginning of the season (September).

2 kg small globe artichokes, trimmed as described opposite
handful of plain flour
500 ml white wine vinegar
about 5 dried bay leaves
1–2 garlic cloves, peeled and left whole, plus 6 garlic cloves, sliced
1 tablespoon table salt
dried mint, oregano and chilli flakes, to taste (optional)
extra-virgin olive oil, to cover

Once you've trimmed the artichokes, immediately place them in a bowl of cold water with the flour (this prevents them from oxidising).

In a saucepan, bring the white wine vinegar, 1 litre of water, 1–2 bay leaves, the whole garlic cloves and salt to the boil. Once boiling, drop in the artichokes. When the mixture returns to the boil, cook the artichokes for 2–5 minutes or until tender.

Drain the artichokes and allow to cool overnight (just leave them in the colander). The next morning, place the artichokes in clean jars (see steps 1–2, page 21) and divide the sliced garlic and remaining bay leaves among them. You could also add dried mint, oregano or chilli flakes, if desired. Completely cover with oil, then seal.

Store in a cool, dark place for at least 2 months before eating. The artichokes will keep for up to 1 year unopened. Once opened, store in the fridge, where they will keep for up to 1 month.

'Just after I was married in 1976, I took my new bride to Italy to meet my relatives. We went to my ancestral village, filled with majestic olive groves and crumbling centuries-old buildings that lined the cobbled, uneven and haphazard streets. Lynn and I spent evenings with my family all huddled together under a blanket by the *braciere*, a copper dish that is filled with embers (this was the only method of heating in the cold winter months). We ate walnuts and talked about my parents and grandparents, and the endless history of the village, going back to Greek occupation. At the end of the evening, our legs and laps were overcooked and our ears and hands freezing, but no one cared.

When we left the village to continue with our travels in our trusty campervan, we were laden with gifts of *capocolli*, salami, jars of sauce and many varieties of vegetables *sott'olio*. We groaned our way north towards Paestum, north of Naples. On the first night, we camped at an isolated *campeggio* (camp site). No hot water, no electricity and not one other camper on site. But next to us, for as far as the eye could see, there were fields of *carciofi* (globe artichokes). In the centre of the field, like the Excalibur, rose a majestic and sacred Greek temple. The local farmers were both respectful of the relics and conscious of the need to conserve them as they circled them on their tractors, while harvesting food from the land as it had been done for more than 4,000 years.'

Globe artichokes, Tuscan style

Carciofi alla Toscana

3 kg globe artichokes, trimmed
    (see page 41 for instructions)
handful of plain flour
1 litre dry white wine
1.5 litres white wine vinegar
handful of flat-leaf parsley sprigs
1–2 dried bay leaves
1½ tablespoons table salt
2 cinnamon sticks
5 cloves
20 whole black peppercorns
extra-virgin olive oil, to cover

Once you've trimmed the artichokes, immediately place them in a bowl of cold water with the flour (this prevents them from oxidising).

Combine the wine, vinegar, parsley, bay leaves and salt in a large stockpot and bring to the boil. Once boiling, add the artichokes and cook for 10 minutes.

Drain the artichokes and, while still hot, divide among clean jars (see steps 1–2, page 21), along with the cinnamon sticks, cloves and peppercorns. Cover with oil, ensuring the artichokes are completely submerged. Seal.

Store in a cool, dark place for at least 2 months before eating. The artichokes will keep for up to 1 year unopened. Once opened, store in the fridge, where they will keep for up to 1 month.

Scottish Thistles (*carciofi Selvatici*) 'Can you believe that those thistles that grow so exuberantly along the sides of the roads and in cemeteries are actually wonderful to eat? In times when food was scarce in Italy, these common weeds became a delicacy, and they can be used in the same way as artichokes. If you happen to find some young ones – and can deal with the headache of preparing them for cooking! – then simply cook in vinegar and water, place in jars with brine and flavourings (garlic, bay leaves and so on) and seal. In a few months you'll have a preserve that tastes just like artichokes!'

Other vegetables

Zucchini in oil

Zucchini sott'olio

In an ideal world, you would use zucchini picked fresh from your garden (or a friend's!). Freshness makes all the difference to the quality of your preserves. When buying zucchini, look for firm fruit with glossy skin and no blemishes.

Preserving zucchini this way helps it stay very crunchy, so it's a pleasure to eat in terms of taste and texture. You can also add sliced carrot, red capsicum, celery or green tomato to the zucchini mixture.

10 zucchini, cut lengthways into 3–4 mm
    thick strips
200 g table salt
500 ml white wine vinegar
5 garlic cloves, finely chopped
4 tablespoons dried oregano
chilli powder or chopped long red chilli,
    to taste (optional)
extra-virgin olive oil, to cover

Special equipment
plastic tub
10 kg weight (about 4 bricks is ideal)

Place the zucchini in layers in the plastic tub, sprinkling each layer liberally with the salt. Position a plate or wooden tray on top of the zucchini, then place a 10 kg weight on top. Leave for 24 hours.

Remove the weights and loosen the zucchini strips with your hands (they should be slightly dry). Add the white wine vinegar and mix thoroughly. Allow to stand for 1 hour, then replace the plate or tray and weight and leave for a further 12 hours.

Drain off the excess vinegar, squeeze the strips dry by hand and place in a bowl with the garlic, oregano and chilli (if using).

Pour a splash of olive oil into a clean jar (see steps 1–2, page 21), then add enough zucchini mixture to almost fill the jar, adding a small amount of olive oil between each layer, to ensure that the oil is evenly distributed. Finally, press down firmly and cover with oil, ensuring the zucchini is completely submerged. Seal. Repeat with as many jars as you need.

Store in a cool, dark place and check after 2–3 days to ensure the oil level hasn't dropped too much. If it has, top it up. The zucchini will keep for up to 1 year unopened and is ready to eat after 1 month. Once opened, store in the fridge, where it will keep for up to 1 month.

Chokos in oil

Zucche spinose sott'olio

The combination of sweet choko and onion makes this a delicate *sott'olio* that is great served as part of an antipasto. You can easily double or triple this recipe if you have a glut of chokos – just remember to use one onion for every three chokos. Also, when slicing the chokos, be sure to wear gloves – the juice is so tart it might peel the skin off your hands!

3 chokos, cut lengthways into 3–4 mm
    thick strips
1 red onion, finely sliced
250 g table salt
500 ml white wine vinegar
5 dried bay leaves
extra-virgin olive oil, to cover

Special equipment
plastic tub
10 kg weight (about 4 bricks is ideal)

Place the choko and onion in layers in the plastic tub, sprinkling each layer liberally with the salt. Position a plate or wooden tray over them and place a 10 kg weight on top. Leave for 24 hours.

Remove the weights and loosen the choko and onion mixture with your hands (it should be slightly dry). Add the white wine vinegar and mix thoroughly. Allow to stand for an hour, then replace the plate or tray and weight and leave for a further 12 hours.

Drain off the excess vinegar, squeeze the strips dry by hand and place them in a clean jar (see steps 1–2, page 21) with the bay leaves. Completely cover with oil and seal.

Store in a cool, dark place for at least 1 month before eating. The chokos will keep for up to 1 year unopened. Once opened, store in the fridge, where they will keep for up to 1 month.

Variation

Mix the chokos with finely sliced red capsicum and carrot rather than onion. After the vinegar stage, add sliced garlic, dried oregano and chopped long red chilli to taste before preserving in oil.

Green tomatoes in vinegar and oil

Pomodori verdi sott'aceto e olio

Choose only the freshest and greenest tomatoes for this preserve, which can be simply eaten with bread or used in a green salad. Green tomatoes make a fantastic, crunchy and unusual antipasto – and this is a great way to use up all the tomatoes at the end of the season.

5 kg green tomatoes, cut into 5 mm thick slices
500 g table salt
500 ml white wine vinegar
4 tablespoons dried oregano
5–6 garlic cloves, finely sliced
2 long red chillies, finely chopped
extra-virgin olive oil, to cover

Special equipment
plastic tub
10 kg weight (about 4 bricks is ideal)

Place the green tomato in the plastic tub and cover liberally with the salt. Position a plate or wooden tray on top of the tomato and place a 10 kg weight on top. Leave for 24 hours.

Remove the weights. Drain off any liquid and gently wash off the excess salt. Cover the tomato with the vinegar, mix well and replace the plate or tray and weight. Leave for a further 24 hours, then drain off the liquid again.

Squeeze the tomato well with your hands, then place it back in the plastic tub, adding the oregano, garlic and chilli. Add a little oil to the mixture and mix well.

Divide the tomato mixture among clean jars (see steps 1–2, page 21) and cover with oil, ensuring the tomato mixture is completely submerged. Seal and leave in a cool, dark place for 1 week, then check the oil level and top up to cover the tomato, if necessary. Leave the tomato in a cool, dark place for another 4–6 weeks before eating. It will keep for up to 1 year unopened. Once opened, store in the fridge, where it will keep for up to 1 month – though you will definitely finish the jar before then!

Mixed vegetables in oil

Giardiniera sott'olio

2 litres white wine vinegar
3 tablespoons sugar
2 dried bay leaves
1 teaspoon table salt
500 g carrots, cut lengthways into 1 cm
    thick batons
200 g celery (use the thick white part at the
    bottom of the bunch), cut into 1 cm pieces
200 g cauliflower, cut into small florets
200 g small pickling onions, peeled and
    left whole
250 g green beans, trimmed and halved (if long)
300 g green tomatoes, cut into 1 cm thick slices
500 g capsicums (any colour), cut lengthways
    into 1 cm thick strips
1 cucumber, cut lengthways into 1 cm
    thick batons
4 garlic cloves, finely sliced
2 tablespoons dried oregano
chilli powder, to taste
extra-virgin olive oil, to cover

In a large stockpot, combine the vinegar, sugar, bay leaves, salt and 1 litre of water and bring to the boil. Lower the carrot, celery, cauliflower, onions and beans into the boiling mixture and allow to boil for 3 minutes. Add the tomato, capsicum and cucumber and boil for a further 2 minutes. This will ensure the vegetables are cooked to the same level of tenderness.

Drain the vegetables and, while they are still hot, place in clean jars (see steps 1–2, page 21). Add the garlic, oregano and chilli powder to taste and cover with oil, ensuring the vegetables are completely submerged but there is still a 2 cm gap at the top of the jars. Screw on the lids and seal the jars hermetically (see page 21) in a hot water bath for 20 minutes to ensure they are airtight.

Store in a cool, dark place for at least 1 month before eating. The vegetables will keep for up to 1 year unopened. Once opened, store in the fridge, where they will keep for up to 1 month.

Cauliflower in oil

Cavolfiore sott'olio

300 g table salt
3 kg cauliflower, cut into small florets
1.5 litres white wine vinegar
10 whole white peppercorns
1 cinnamon stick
peel of 1 lemon
3 dried bay leaves, plus 1 extra per jar
extra-virgin olive oil, to cover

Dissolve the salt in 3 litres of water and soak the cauliflower florets in this mixture for 2 hours. This will prime it for preservation as well as remove any dirt or pests!

In a large stockpot, combine the vinegar, white peppercorns, cinnamon stick, lemon peel and three bay leaves and bring to the boil. Add the cauliflower florets and boil for 5 minutes, then drain and arrange in clean jars (see steps 1–2, page 21). Add an extra bay leaf to each jar, then cover with oil, ensuring the cauliflower is completely submerged.

Leave for 1 day, uncovered, then check the oil level and top up to cover the cauliflower, if necessary. Seal and store in a cool, dark place for at least 1 month before eating. It will keep for up to 1 year. Once opened, store the cauliflower in the fridge, where it will keep for up to 1 month.

Gherkins in oil

Cetriolini sott'olio

3 kg small gherkins, left whole
650 g coarse sea salt
4–5 dried bay leaves
4–5 basil leaves
4 garlic cloves, finely sliced
3 long red chillies, finely sliced
10 whole black peppercorns
2 litres white wine vinegar
250 ml white wine
extra-virgin olive oil, to cover

Special equipment
plastic tub

Place the gherkins in the plastic tub, cover with the salt and leave for 48 hours. Drain and divide among clean jars (see steps 1–2, page 21). Distribute the bay leaves, basil, garlic, chilli and black peppercorns evenly among the jars.

In a large stockpot, combine the vinegar and wine and bring to the boil. Once boiling, immediately (and carefully) pour the hot liquid into the jars, ensuring the vegetables are fully covered. Seal the jars immediately and allow to stand for 10 days.

After 10 days, drain the pickling liquid out of the jars, leaving the gherkins, herbs and garlic in the jars. Completely cover with oil and allow to stand overnight, uncovered, before sealing.

Store in a cool, dark place for at least 1 month before eating. The gherkins will keep for up to 1 year unopened. Once opened, store in the fridge, where they will keep for up to 1 month.

Beans in oil

Fagiolini sott'olio

1 litre white wine vinegar
table salt
2 kg green beans, trimmed
5 dried bay leaves
4 sage leaves
1 garlic clove, finely sliced
freshly ground black pepper, to taste
extra-virgin olive oil, to cover

Bring the vinegar and 500 ml of water to the boil in a large stockpot. Add salt to taste, as if you were preparing to cook pasta, then plunge the beans into the boiling mixture. Cook for 5 minutes, then drain.

Following the instructions on page 21, arrange the beans vertically in clean jars, then distribute the bay leaves, sage, garlic and black pepper among the jars. Completely cover with oil, leaving a 2 cm gap at the top of the jars. Screw on the lids, then hermetically seal the jars in a hot water bath for 20 minutes to ensure they are airtight.

Store in a cool, dark place for at least 1 month before eating. The beans will keep for up to 1 year unopened. Once opened, store them in the fridge, where they will keep for up to 1 month.

Variation

You can also add the beans, garlic and herbs to the water while it's still cold and then drain the beans once the mixture comes to boiling point. This just creates a different texture – some think the beans are crispier this way!

VEGETABLES IN VINEGAR

CONSERVE SOTT'ACETO

02

All vegetables can be preserved in vinegar. This forms the basis of the traditional Italian *giardiniera* (see page 54).

When using vinegar, it is important to boil it first as this will sterilise the vinegar and prevent any chance of mould or spoilage. To seal hermetically, always pour the vinegar and spices directly from boiling point into your jars of vegetables, then immediately seal the jars. This ensures that the vinegar is sterile, and the jars will form an airtight seal as the vinegar cools. As always, you will notice a few variations to these 'rules' in the recipes to follow, as everyone has their own way, but these are the basic principles.

As with preserving *sott'olio*, the fresher your vegetables are, the better the quality of your preserve. The amount of herbs, chilli and other flavourings given in the following recipes should be used as a guide only. Let your own tastes determine the amounts – if you like it hot, add more chilli!

Vegetables in vinegar

Giardiniera sott'aceto

These are always served at the beginning of a meal with a slice of prosciutto or salami. The vinegar stimulates the salivary glands and improves your digestion (and appreciation!) of the food.

2 teaspoons table salt, plus extra to taste
500 g carrots, sliced into 5 mm thick batons
500 g celery (use the thick white part
    at the bottom of the bunch), sliced into
    2 cm pieces
500 g small pickling onions, peeled and
    left whole
500 g cauliflower, sliced into small florets
300 g green beans, trimmed and sliced into
    2 cm long pieces
300 g green tomatoes, cut into 5 mm
    thick slices
200 g red or green capsicums, sliced into
    2 cm strips
2 firm cucumbers, sliced into 5 mm thick batons
1.5 litres white wine vinegar
2–3 cloves
freshly grated nutmeg, to taste
20 whole black peppercorns
4 dried bay leaves
2 garlic cloves, finely sliced
1–2 long red chillies, sliced

In a large stockpot, bring the salt and 2 litres of water to the boil. Lower the carrot, celery, onions and cauliflower into the boiling mixture and allow to boil for 2–3 minutes. Add the beans, tomato, capsicum and cucumber and boil for a further 1–2 minutes. This will ensure the vegetables are cooked to the same level of tenderness. Once ready, drain the vegetables and allow to cool.

In the same stockpot, combine the white wine vinegar with 1 litre of water, the spices, bay leaves, garlic, chilli and salt to taste. Alternatively, you can leave out the spices (as they do with commercially produced *giardiniera*), but surely that is the fun of making your own?

Bring the vinegar mixture to the boil, leave to boil for 5 minutes and then cool slightly.

Following the instructions on page 21, distribute the vegetables among clean jars and completely cover with the spicy vinegar mix, leaving a 2 cm gap at the top of the jars. Hermetically seal the jars in a hot water bath for 20 minutes to ensure they are airtight, then store them in a cool, dark place for 3–4 weeks before eating. The vegetables will keep for up to 1 year unopened. Once opened, store them in the fridge, where they will keep for up to 1 month.

Variation

Rosetta's pickled vegetables
Giardiniera di Rosetta

Follow the recipe above but instead of boiling the vegetables in salted water, place them in a plastic tub and cover with salt (approximately 1 kg of salt per 5 kg of vegetables) for 24 hours, as for *sott'olio*. The next day, wash off the excess salt and prepare the hot vinegar as per the recipe above, but just use sugar and bay leaves rather than the extra spices suggested. Place extra bay leaves in clean jars (see steps 1–2, page 21) with the vegetables, and completely cover with the vinegar mix, leaving a 2 cm gap at the top of the jars. Hermetically seal and store as above.

Cauliflower in vinegar

Cavolfiore sott'aceto

200 g table salt
2 kg cauliflower, cut into small florets
1 litre white wine vinegar
juice of 1 lemon
2–3 dried bay leaves
whole black peppercorns, to taste
table salt, to taste

Dissolve the salt in 2 litres of water and soak the cauliflower in this mixture for 2 hours. This will prime it for preservation as well as remove any dirt or pests.

Drain the cauliflower. Bring a large stockpot of water to the boil and cook the cauliflower for 2–3 minutes or until tender. Drain and rinse the cauliflower under cold running water to prevent it cooking further. Drain again and place in clean jars (see steps 1–2, page 21).

Combine the vinegar, lemon juice, bay leaves, peppercorns and salt to taste in a large saucepan. Bring to the boil, allow to simmer for 2–3 minutes, then turn off the heat and let it cool slightly.

Pour the still hot vinegar mixture into the jars, ensuring the cauliflower is completely submerged but there is still a 2 cm gap at the top of the jars. Screw on the lids; the jars will seal hermetically as the vinegar cools.

Store in a cool, dark place for at least 1 month before eating. The cauliflower will keep for up to 1 year unopened. Once opened, store in the fridge, where it will keep for up to 1 month.

Cucumbers in vinegar

Cetrioli sott'aceto

You can also use Lebanese cucumbers for this recipe; they are slightly larger than pickling cucumbers.

1 kg small pickling cucumbers
4–5 small pickling onions, peeled and left whole
3–4 cloves
10–15 whole black peppercorns
freshly grated nutmeg, to taste
1–2 long red chillies, finely sliced
1–2 dried bay leaves
1 teaspoon table salt
500 ml white wine vinegar

Place the cucumbers and onions in clean jars (see steps 1–2, page 21). Add the spices, chilli, bay leaves and salt.

Bring the vinegar to the boil, then pour immediately into the jars, ensuring the vegetables are completely submerged but there is still a 2 cm gap at the top of the jars. Screw on the lids. The jars will seal hermetically as the vinegar cools.

Store the cucumbers in the fridge for 3–4 weeks before eating; they will keep for up to 6 months in the fridge.

Gherkins in vinegar

Cetriolini sott'aceto

3 kg gherkins, washed and dried
100 g table salt
1 litre white wine vinegar
10 whole black peppercorns
4 cloves
long red chillies, sliced or left whole, to taste
1–2 dried bay leaves

Special equipment
plastic tub

Place the gherkins in the plastic tub, cover with the salt, then leave for 24 hours.

The next day, wash off the excess salt thoroughly and place the gherkins in a large saucepan or heatproof bowl.

In a stockpot, bring the white wine vinegar, black peppercorns, cloves, chilli and bay leaves to the boil. Remove from the heat and pour over the gherkins.

Allow to cool and leave, covered, for 24 hours.

The next day, drain the gherkins, reserving the vinegar. Place the gherkins in clean jars (see steps 1–2, page 21). Re-boil the reserved vinegar mixture and pour over the gherkins, ensuring they are completely submerged but there is still a 2 cm gap at the top of the jars. Seal the jars immediately; they will seal hermetically as the vinegar mixture cools.

Store the gherkins in the fridge for 3–4 weeks before eating; they will keep for up to 6 months in the fridge.

Small onions in vinegar

Cipolline sott'aceto

The small onions you want for this recipe are sometimes referred to as pickling onions.

2 kg small pickling onions, peeled and left whole
table salt
1 litre white wine vinegar, plus extra for soaking
100 g caster sugar
20 whole black peppercorns
4 dried bay leaves

Place the onions in a large saucepan or heatproof bowl full of salted water that has been acidulated with 2–3 tablespoons of white wine vinegar. Allow to soak for 5 minutes, then drain and dry the onions with a clean tea towel.

In a stockpot, bring the 1 litre of white wine vinegar, the sugar, peppercorns, bay leaves and salt to taste to the boil. Allow to boil for 1 minute.

Place the onions in clean jars (see steps 1–2, page 21) and pour the hot vinegar over them, ensuring they are completely submerged but there is still a 2 cm gap at the top of the jars. Seal the jars immediately; they will seal hermetically as the vinegar mixture cools.

Store the onions in the fridge for 1 month before eating; they will keep for up to 6 months in the fridge.

Green beans in vinegar

Fagiolini freschi sott'aceto

2 kg green beans, trimmed and halved (if long)
table salt
500 ml white wine vinegar
2–4 cloves
2 teaspoons dried tarragon

Cook the beans in salted boiling water for 5 minutes or until tender (but still a bit crunchy). Drain and set aside to cool slightly.

In another saucepan, combine the white wine vinegar, cloves, tarragon and 1 tablespoon of salt. Bring to the boil over high heat and allow to boil for 1 minute.

Place the cooked beans upright in clean jars (see steps 1–2, page 21) and pour over the hot vinegar, ensuring they are completely submerged but there is still a 2 cm gap at the top of the jars. Seal the jars immediately; they will seal hermetically as the vinegar mixture cools.

Store the beans in the fridge for 3–4 weeks before eating; they will keep for up to 6 months in the fridge.

Capsicums in vinegar

Peperoni sott'aceto

This recipe is for the smaller bell capsicums you can buy and leave whole, which are perfect for pickling. Ensure you select very firm and shiny capsicums as they will hold their shape better.

1 litre white wine vinegar
1 teaspoon table salt
2–3 dried bay leaves
2–3 long red chillies, finely sliced
10 whole black peppercorns
3 kg red or green small (or pickling) bell capsicums, left whole

Combine the vinegar, salt, bay leaves, chilli and black peppercorns in a large stockpot, then bring to the boil. Drop the capsicums in (carefully) and cook for 2–3 minutes, then remove, reserving the vinegar mixture.

Place the capsicums in clean jars (see steps 1–2, page 21). Cover with the hot vinegar mixture, ensuring they are completely submerged but there is still a 2 cm gap at the top of the jars. Seal the jars immediately; they will seal hermetically as the vinegar mixture cools.

Store the capsicums in the fridge for 3–4 weeks before eating; they will keep for up to 6 months in the fridge.

Hot chillies in vinegar

Peperoncini sott'aceto

1 kg long red and green chillies, left whole
1 litre white wine vinegar
garlic cloves, peeled and left whole
    (you'll need 2–3 per jar)
table salt, to taste

Place the chillies in small clean jars (see steps 1–2, page 21). If they are long chillies, arrange them upright.

Heat the vinegar to boiling point, then pour it into the jars, ensuring the chillies are completely submerged but there is still a 2 cm gap at the top of the jars. Add two or three cloves of garlic to each jar, plus salt to taste, then seal the jars while the vinegar is still hot. The jars will seal hermetically as the vinegar mixture cools.

Store the chillies in the fridge for 3–4 weeks before eating; they will keep for up to 6 months in the fridge.

Eggplants in vinegar

Melanzane sott'aceto

2 kg eggplants, sliced lengthways into
    5 mm thick strips
200 g table salt
juice of 1 lemon
500 ml white wine vinegar
10 dried bay leaves
10 flat-leaf parsley sprigs
20 whole black peppercorns

Special equipment
plastic tub

Place the eggplant in the plastic tub and cover liberally with the salt. Allow to stand for 12 hours, then drain off any liquid.

Fill a large stockpot with water, add the lemon juice and bring the mixture to the boil. Carefully add the salted eggplant strips and when the mixture returns to the boil, immediately remove from the heat and drain the eggplant. Dry with a clean tea towel if necessary, removing any excess liquid. Place the eggplant in clean jars (see steps 1–2, page 21).

In a separate pot (or just clean the one you used before), combine the vinegar, bay leaves, parsley and peppercorns and bring to the boil. Once the mixture is boiling, turn off the heat and allow to cool slightly.

Pour the still hot vinegar mixture over the eggplant strips, ensuring they are completely submerged but there is still a 2 cm gap at the top of the jars. Seal the jars immediately; they will seal hermetically as the vinegar mixture cools.

Store in a cool, dark place for at least 1 month before eating. The eggplant will keep for up to 1 year unopened. Once opened, store in the fridge, where it will keep for up to 1 month.

Celery in vinegar

Sedano sott'aceto

When preserving celery, don't let any of it go to waste. Reserve the leaves for salads, keep the thicker white ends for stocks or *giardiniera* (see pages 46 and 54) and use the thinner green stalks to make the most attractive preserve, as follows.

2 teaspoons table salt
2 teaspoons whole black peppercorns
2 dried bay leaves
2 cloves
2 kg celery, sliced into 5 cm long sticks
juice of 1 lemon
2 garlic cloves, peeled and left whole
2 basil leaves
2 litres white wine vinegar

In a large stockpot, combine the salt, black peppercorns, bay leaves and cloves with 3 litres of water and bring to the boil. Carefully drop in the celery sticks and allow to cook until the water returns to boiling point, then remove from the heat and drain the celery, reserving the peppercorns, bay leaves and cloves.

Place the celery sticks in two clean jars (see steps 1–2, page 21), together with the lemon juice, a garlic clove, a basil leaf, a bay leaf, a clove and a few peppercorns per jar.

Bring the white wine vinegar to the boil and allow to cool slightly before pouring over the celery, ensuring the pieces are fully submerged but there is still a 2 cm gap at the top of the jars. Seal the jars immediately; they will seal hermetically as the vinegar mixture cools.

Store in the fridge for 3–4 weeks before eating; the celery will keep for up to 6 months in the fridge.

Sweet pickled vegetables

Verdure agrodolci

1 litre white wine vinegar
80 g caster sugar
1 teaspoon table salt
1 kg mixed vegetables, such as carrot sticks,
    small picking onions (peeled and left whole),
    cauliflower florets, celery sticks, green beans
    (trimmed and left whole), sliced tomato,
    peas, sliced capsicum and sliced small
    pickling cucumbers

In a large stockpot, bring 1.25 litres of water, the vinegar, sugar and salt to the boil.

Lower the carrot, onions, cauliflower and celery into the boiling mixture and allow to boil for 2–3 minutes. Add the beans, tomato, peas, capsicum and cucumber and boil for a further 1–2 minutes. This will ensure the vegetables are cooked to the same level of tenderness. Once ready, drain the vegetables (reserving the vinegar) and allow to cool.

Place the vegetables on a large baking tray to cool and dry out overnight.

The next day, arrange an attractive mixture of vegetables among clean jars (see steps 1–2, page 21). Reheat the reserved vinegar mixture to boiling point, then pour over the vegetables, ensuring they are completely submerged but there is still a 2 cm gap at the top of the jars. Seal the jars immediately; they will seal hermetically as the vinegar mixture cools.

Store in the fridge for 1 month before eating; the vegetables will keep for up to 6 months in the fridge.

Sweet pickled green beans

Fagiolini freschi agrodolci

Select young, fresh beans for this recipe. Ideal if you have a glut of them growing in your garden!

2 litres white wine vinegar
250 g sugar
2 cloves
table salt, to taste
2 kg green beans, trimmed and sliced into
    3 cm lengths
dried bay leaves (you'll need 1 per jar)

In a large stockpot, bring the vinegar, sugar, cloves and salt to taste to the boil. Add the beans and cook for 2 minutes.

Carefully remove the beans with a slotted spoon or tongs and place in clean jars (see steps 1–2, page 21). Pour over the hot vinegar mixture, ensuring the beans are completely submerged but there is still a 2 cm gap at the top of the jars. Add a bay leaf to each jar, then seal immediately; the jars will seal hermetically as the vinegar mixture cools.

Store in the fridge for 1 month before eating; the beans will keep for up to 6 months in the fridge.

Perfumed globe artichokes

Carciofi profumati

These are superb in a salad or on a pizza.

2 litres white wine vinegar
3 garlic cloves
200 ml freshly squeezed lemon juice
3–4 cloves
1 teaspoon cumin seeds
1 thyme sprig
freshly ground black pepper, to taste
2 tablespoons table salt
4 kg globe artichokes, trimmed
    (see page 41 for instructions)

Place all the ingredients, except the artichokes, in a stockpot with 3 litres of water and bring to the boil.

Once boiling, drop in the artichokes and boil for 5 minutes.

Remove the artichokes with a slotted spoon, reserving the cooking liquid. While still hot, arrange the artichokes in clean jars (see steps 1–2, page 21), adding enough of the reserved cooking liquid to completely cover but leaving a 2 cm gap at the top of the jars.

Hermetically seal the jars (see page 21) in a hot water bath for 20 minutes to ensure they are airtight, then store in a cool, dark place for up to 1 year. They will be ready to eat after 3–4 weeks. Once opened, the artichokes will keep in the fridge for up to 3 months.

FUNGI

FUNGHI

03

Many years ago, while we were renovating our home and experiencing the usual frustrating months of waiting for different contractors, the heating technician arrived to install our new bathroom heater. Once he was finished, we began talking about preserving foods. He was very proud of his recipe for preserved field mushrooms. 'Where do you find them?' I asked. 'In the hills around Melbourne, under pine trees!' was his reply.

The next morning at 6 am, a drizzly and cold Sunday, we set off with him to the hills. For the first three hours, we stumbled around from pine tree to pine tree until finally he found what he was looking for: a largish mushroom that was bright orange and slightly concave upwards. This was the *Lactarius Deliciosus* that he had been picking in Italy and here in Australia for many years. The children were ecstatic. It reminded them (and me) of our mushroom-picking adventures in Italy when, with our friend Ciccio, we picked 40 kilograms of the very same mushrooms in the fields between Florence and Bologna.

The flavour and texture of wild mushrooms is so exquisite that they are absolutely worth the effort of collecting, but it is most important that you know exactly what you are picking. It is possible to find excellent wild mushrooms in Australia, but you must be careful. Always go with someone who knows what they're looking for and can advise you on what is safe to eat. Ask your plumber or electrician – you never know!

Wild mushrooms in oil

Funghi selvatici sott'olio

I find that extra-virgin olive oil is too strongly flavoured for mushrooms and tends to drown their delicate earthiness. Therefore, I recommend using a light olive oil, or even a good-quality vegetable oil, for this recipe.

When picking mushrooms, always leave the stem of the mushroom in the ground. This will provide the spores for next year's crop. Also, remember that mushrooms should never be washed with water, but rather gently wiped or brushed clean.

It is tricky to give exact quantities for the other ingredients because, of course, it will depend on how many mushrooms you collect! As a rough guide, make a mixture of one part white wine vinegar and three parts water with salt to taste (approximately 2 tablespoons for every 4 litres of water).

white wine vinegar
table salt
wild field mushrooms, wiped or brushed clean,
    left whole
dried oregano
garlic cloves
light olive oil, to cover

In a large stockpot, combine the vinegar, water and salt to taste and bring to the boil. Carefully drop in the mushrooms and cook for 3 minutes.

Drain the mushrooms and allow them to dry as much as possible before you place them under oil. Our heating technician told us his wife places them in a calico bag and puts them through a spin cycle in the washing machine! Another method is to place the mushrooms between two clean tea towels in the sink and place a weight (roughly 2 kg) on top, then leave overnight.

Following the instructions on page 21, place the mushrooms in clean jars, with the oregano and garlic (you could also add mint, bay leaves or chopped chilli). Pour in the olive oil, ensuring the mushrooms are completely covered but there is still a 2 cm gap at the top of the jars. Screw on the lids. Hermetically seal the jars in a hot water bath for 40 minutes to ensure they are airtight.

Store in a cool, dark place for 3–4 weeks before eating. The mushrooms will keep for up to 1 year unopened. Once opened, store them in the fridge, where they will keep for up to 1 month.

Dried mushrooms

Funghi secchi

You can make this recipe with field mushrooms you've picked yourself or with store-bought mushrooms. These dried mushrooms are excellent added to *sugo* (sauce) or in casseroles or soup. You could also try adding a couple to a pasta dish made with garlic, oil, chopped flat-leaf parsley and chillies to make an '*aglio olio e peperoncini*' with a difference.

If you have a dehydrator, then this will be very easy. Otherwise, mushrooms can be dried in an oven. Use them any time you need the delicate flavour of mushrooms. You can also pulverise the dried mushrooms in a food processor to produce a powder.

field mushrooms, wiped or brushed clean
and cut into 1 cm thick slices

Preheat the oven to 80°C fan-forced.

Spread the mushroom slices evenly over baking trays (there is no need to grease or line them) and place in the preheated oven for 12 hours. If you feel comfortable you can do this overnight.

Once dry, place the mushroom pieces in clean jars (see steps 1–2, page 21) and seal until needed. They will keep for up to 2 years in a cool, dark place.

'Some time ago, we had a *commare* in our village who went mushroom picking and cooked up a great feast of field mushrooms for her family. The *commare* threw the scraps to the chickens and some time later noticed that all the chickens were lying on the ground with their feet in the air. The mushrooms must have been poisonous! She and her family all rushed to the hospital and had their stomachs pumped, returning home many hours later, tired and stressed. The *commare* went out to bury the chickens, only to find they were all healthy and running around! It turned out that the mushrooms had a short-acting relaxant effect on the chickens, from which they totally recovered ... which is more than I can say for the *commare*. She has never eaten a mushroom since!'

'Ciccio Tarsia is a very special friend I met in Florence in 1986.
He comes from Cosenza in Calabria. We bonded instantly over
our mutual love for traditional food, even though we had never met
before. At the time he was doing a three-year course in the study of fungi
(mycology), and was a member of both the Slow Food Society in Italy
and the International Hot Chilli Association. He was also a prolific
producer of traditional preserves. His dream was to own a small farm
in Tuscany, where he would have his own vines and olive trees and raise
his own pigs. He achieved this in 1996 when he moved to Cavriglia, south
of Florence on the border of Tuscany and Umbria, where he bought
and restored an 11th century abbey cellar and opened a restaurant,
Papposileno, which is still going strong today!

When the restaurant first opened, I flew over from Australia
to join in the festivities (and help out during his busy first week). By the
second night, I was officially both waiter and maître d'! Coincidentally,
at one of my tables was an Australian couple from Melbourne. It was
a fantastic experience, but I did not give the encounter another thought.
On my first day back at my surgery in Melbourne, one of my staff
remarked: "I hear you were working as a waiter in Italy!" It turned out
the couple I looked after were the parents of her daughter's boyfriend.
An incredible coincidence, but it just goes to show that even if you are
25,000 kilometres away, in a tiny village in rural Italy, on the second
opening night of a small restaurant, you never know who might
be there! Misbehave and you'll be found out.

On that trip, Ciccio and I walked through the dense pine
forests of Tuscany looking for the red pine mushrooms that the Italians
call *pennenciole*. These are also found in the Mornington Peninsula,
in Victoria, and are called *Lactarius Deliciosus*. Ciccio also taught me the
gentle and patient art of searching for the prized porcini mushrooms
and the tiny *chiodini* (little nails) at the base of small cypress-like shrubs.
Once home, we cooked, pickled, salted and dried the mushrooms
for use later on. No one knows mushrooms quite like Ciccio and
I am pleased to share some of his recipes here.'

Mushrooms in brine

Funghi sotto sale

When mushrooms are readily available all year round, I appreciate it may not seem worthwhile to preserve them. But it is such a pleasure to collect your own field mushrooms and keep them all year. Preserved in this way, these mushrooms can be added to salads and omelettes for a taste of the forest.

1 litre white wine vinegar
300 g wild field mushrooms (preferably)
    or small store-bought field mushrooms,
    wiped or brushed clean, left whole
300 g table salt

Special equipment
large, wide-mouthed ceramic jar
wooden disc (the same size as the
    opening of the ceramic jar)
5 kg weight (about 2 bricks is ideal)

In a large stockpot, combine the vinegar with 500 ml of water and bring to the boil. Carefully drop in the mushrooms and cook for 3 minutes. Drain the mushrooms and allow to dry overnight on a clean tea towel.

The next day, make a brine by bringing the salt and 1 litre of water to the boil in a large stockpot. Pour the brine into the ceramic jar.

Place the mushrooms in the brine and submerge them under the wooden disc, then place a 5 kg weight on top and cover. Allow the mushrooms to remain under brine until you need to use them. When you want to eat them, rinse in clean water three times and then soak in more clean water for 3 hours. They can be eaten immediately or stored in a cool, dark place for 2–3 months.

Button mushrooms in vinegar

Funghetti coltivati sott'aceto

This recipe is ideal for those small button mushrooms you find in the supermarket.

2 teaspoons table salt
juice of 1 lemon
2 kg small button mushrooms, wiped or
    brushed clean, left whole
1.5 litres white wine vinegar
2 cloves
1 cinnamon stick
light olive oil, to seal
handful of tarragon leaves
10 whole black peppercorns

In a large stockpot, combine 3 litres of water with the salt and lemon juice and bring to the boil. Carefully drop in the mushrooms and wait until the mixture comes to the boil again, then turn off the heat and drain the mushrooms. Place them in clean jars (see steps 1–2, page 21) while you prepare the vinegar.

Heat the vinegar, cloves and cinnamon stick in a stockpot until boiling. Take off the heat and allow to cool slightly before removing the whole spices and pouring the still hot vinegar over the mushrooms, ensuring they are completely submerged but there is still a 2 cm gap at the top of the jars.

Add a splash of olive oil to each jar, as well as some tarragon leaves and black peppercorns. Seal the jars while the vinegar mixture is still hot; the jars will seal hermetically as the mixture cools.

Store in the fridge for 1 month before eating; the mushrooms will keep for up to 6 months in the fridge.

Ciccio's mushrooms in oil

Funghi sott'olio di Ciccio

As mentioned previously, I prefer to use light olive oil when preserving mushrooms *sott'olio* as extra-virgin is far too strong and overwhelms their delicate flavour. You could also use a good-quality vegetable oil.

500 ml white wine vinegar
2 teaspoons table salt
2–3 cloves
2 kg button mushrooms, wiped or brushed
    clean and left whole
4 dried bay leaves
10 whole black peppercorns
3 garlic cloves, finely sliced
20 capers
light olive oil, to cover

In a large stockpot, combine the vinegar, salt and cloves with 500 ml of water and bring to the boil. Carefully drop in the mushrooms, allow the mixture to return to the boil and then cook for 5 minutes. Drain and allow the mushrooms to dry overnight on a clean tea towel.

The next day, place the mushrooms in small clean jars (see steps 1–2, page 21) with the bay leaves, black peppercorns, garlic and capers, then cover with light olive oil, ensuring the mushrooms are completely submerged. Seal.

Store in a cool, dark place for up to 1 year. The mushrooms can be eaten immediately. Once opened, store them in the fridge, where they will keep for up to 1 month.

Variation

For *funghi piccanti*, follow the recipe above but add 2 teaspoons of chopped Dried Hot Chillies (see page 109) to the mushrooms before distributing among jars and covering with olive oil. You could also add some dried basil if you like. Allow to stand for 2 months before eating.

Wild mushrooms under oil

Funghi di prato sott'olio

On my farm at Balnarring, April is always an exciting month as we wait for the first wild mushrooms to appear. The amounts vary but we always have slippery jacks and pine mushrooms. Slippery jacks are chestnut brown in colour and have a slimy, wet appearance. The cap is convex when young and tends to flatten out in maturity. Please be cautious whenever picking wild mushrooms – it is vital you know what you're picking and whether it is safe to eat. If in doubt, leave it! You can usually buy them at a farmer's market when they are in season.

I like to call this recipe 'Australian porcinis'! They are delicious on bruschetta, with pasta or in risotto. I haven't provided exact quantities for the ingredients because, again, it will depend on how many mushrooms you collect! Let your taste be the guide.

extra-virgin olive oil, for pan-frying
garlic cloves, finely sliced
slippery jacks and pine mushrooms, wiped
    or brushed clean and cut into 1 cm thick
    strips, slippery jacks peeled
dried tarragon
salt and freshly ground black pepper
light olive oil, to cover

In a large frying pan, heat a splash of extra-virgin olive oil over medium–high heat. Add the garlic and fry for 1 minute until fragrant, then add the mushrooms, tarragon and salt and pepper. Cover with a lid and allow to simmer, stirring occasionally. Initially, the mushrooms will exude a lot of juice. Just turn them over and keep cooking! After 10–15 minutes, the juices will have evaporated. Make sure that all you have left are the mushrooms.

Pour a splash of light olive oil into a clean jar (see steps 1–2, page 21), then almost fill with mushrooms. Cover with light olive oil, ensuring the mushrooms are completely submerged but there is still a 2 cm gap at the top, then screw on the lid. Repeat with as many jars as you need. Hermetically seal the jars (see page 21) in a hot water bath for 40 minutes to ensure they are airtight.

Store in a cool, dark place for 1 month before eating. The mushrooms will keep for up to 1 year unopened. Once opened, store them in the fridge, where they will keep for up to 1 month.

OLIVES

L'OLIVE

Preserving th
Italian Way

by Pietro Demaio

04

Italy is synonymous with the olive tree. As you move further south, these ancient trees reach up higher and higher, their trunks becoming larger and more twisted. Each taking on a form all of their own, over the centuries they have witnessed so many stories of hardship, pleasure, companionship, treachery, honour, love, hate, family struggles and successes. They tell us the whole history of Italy through the ages and under different masters.

On visits to Italy, I have walked through the groves in my parents' village in Varapodio and tried to imagine what it was like for my mother and father before they emigrated to Australia, working almost as slaves under the feudal system, not knowing from one day to the next whether they had work, and always under pressure to feed their ever-growing family in a beautiful but totally unforgiving countryside.

Wherever Italians have migrated, you will find olive trees (admittedly, there are no olives in the Arctic and Antarctic but we are working on that!). All over Australia, Italian homes are distinguishable by their unique blend of beauty and pragmatism – the white balustrades, the brightly coloured rendered fences, the shutter blinds, the fruit trees out in the front garden and, always, the olive tree in the nature strip.

There are some basic rules for preserving olives:

* Always use fresh, hard and unbruised fruit.
* Make sure all your utensils are clean. Do not use copper, brass, iron or galvanised utensils, as this will cause a chemical reaction with the olives and taint the flavour.
* Make sure your containers for brining are clean, unchipped and made from non-reactive materials: glass, stainless steel, enamelware, stoneware, porcelain, earthenware, terracotta or plastic.
* Always clean jars and lids before use (see steps 1–2, page 21).
* Always fill your jars evenly and make sure the olives are completely submerged in the brine. If any olives are above the brine, they will turn brown and soft and taste mouldy.
* Always wipe the rims of the jars well to ensure that the seals are as tight as they can be.
* The basic ratio for preserving olives in brine is 1 kg of olives, 1 litre of water and 100 g of salt.

Olives can be prepared for preserving in a number of ways. The most common are as follows.

Curing in caustic soda

The curing of green olives with lye (a dilute solution of caustic soda) is popular in Central and Northern Italy. There are many varieties and sizes of olives, each of which has a different oil content. The best varieties to use for this method are the sevillano (Spanish queen), ascolani and manzanillo. Manzanillo takes longer to cure with lye. You need to be attentive to the concentration of the lye because if it is too strong, the skin of the olive is liable to blister. The ideal temperature for this process is 18–29°C, with the rate of curing increasing with temperature. Once the olives are cured in this way, they can be placed in brine (see below).

Salt and water (brine)

The brine needs to be 100 g salt per 1 litre of water. Traditionally, you add enough salt to the water to make an egg float! This can still be a useful way of gauging if the water is salty enough, though the measurements above should have you on the right track.

To preserve olives in brine you need acid (lemon or vinegar) and salt (100 g per litre of water). The pickling time will vary depending on the olives' size (longer for larger), ripeness (green take longer than black) and variety (kalamata take up to 3 months and will always remain slightly bitter, while verdale, frantoio and leccino take less time and will taste nuttier and less bitter).

Note that all olives preserved in brine (salt, water and lemon or vinegar) will ferment in the jars – this is the curing process. So when you open a jar after 6–12 weeks it will fizz like a bottle of soda water. This is the carbon dioxide that has formed during the fermentation process – the olives have not gone off! Once opened, the olives can be stored in the fridge for months.

Vinegar and oil

Acid can be added by using vinegar rather than lemon, which is typical of Greek-style olives. Add 250 ml of white wine vinegar for every 1 litre of brine and continue as above. Once cured, store the olives in the brine or drain and completely cover in extra-virgin olive oil, to which you can add flavourings such as dried oregano, chilli or fennel seeds.

Olives cured with caustic soda, the Abruzzi way

Olive all' Abruzzese

7 tablespoons caustic soda
10 kg hard, fresh green olives (ideally the
    Spanish queen variety)
500 g table salt

Special equipment
3 litre plastic bucket
20 litre plastic bucket

In the 3 litre bucket, slowly and very carefully mix 1 litre of water with the caustic soda. The caustic soda will heat up, so stay well away. Dilute the caustic soda solution by pouring it into the 20 litre bucket with another 14 litres of water.

Add the olives and mix well. The olives need to be stirred every hour for the first couple of hours. After a period of 10–24 hours, the olives will settle on the bottom of the bucket and there will be none floating on the surface. The olives are now cured. Very carefully pour off the caustic soda solution, then fill the bucket with fresh water.

A reddish pink liquid will come out of the olives. Keep changing the water daily for a further 6–7 days until the water becomes clear and is no longer pink.

At this stage, the olives are ready to place in brine. If the olives are not washed properly of caustic soda solution, they are likely to have a slightly soapy taste to them. Distribute the olives among clean jars (see steps 1–2, page 21).

In a large stockpot, mix the salt with 5 litres of water and bring to boiling point, then remove from the heat. Boiling the brine sterilises the water and prevents any mould from forming that would spoil the olives. Pour the hot brine over the olives, ensuring they are completely submerged but there is still a 2 cm gap at the top of the jars. Seal; the jars will seal hermetically as they cool. Store in a cool, dark place for 6 weeks before eating. The olives will keep for up to 2 years unopened. Once opened, store in the fridge, where they will keep for up to 6 months.

Olives in brine

Olive in salamoia

This is my *compare* Frank's recipe, following the more traditional method for green olives in Southern Italy, which is to pickle them in brine.

Ensure your olives are perfect – hard and green all over. The best variety to use are Spanish queens, if you can get them.

100 g table salt
1 kg hard, fresh green olives
2 garlic cloves, peeled and left whole
2 small green jalapeno chillies, left whole
2 slices of lemon
1 teaspoon fennel seeds (or wild fennel flowers,
    if you have them available)

Make a brine by bringing the salt and 1 litre of water to the boil in a large stockpot. If you need more brine, add 100 g of table salt for every 1 litre of water.

Distribute the olives between two large clean jars (see steps 1–2, page 21). Add a garlic clove and chilli to each jar, then place a lemon slice on top. If you have access to wild fennel flowers, place a few of these on top too. They not only add flavour but also help to keep the olives submerged in the brine, thus preventing discolouration. Alternatively, you could add fennel seeds for the same flavour.

Pour the still hot brine over the olives, ensuring they are completely submerged but there is still a 2 cm gap at the top of the jars. Seal. As the brine cools, it will seal the jars hermetically to prevent the brine from developing a mould and to keep the olives firm. Store in a cool, dark place for 6 months before eating. The olives will keep for up to 2 years unopened. Once opened, store in the fridge, where they will keep for up to 6 months.

Variation

Some recipes recommend you first soak the olives in a bucket of water, changing the water daily for 3 days. This produces a slightly sweeter end result. You can also add sliced celery or extra lemon slices to vary the flavour. I personally like the original recipe.

Olives in oil

Olive sott'olio

When you have eaten all of these olives, make sure you use the leftover oil – either for cooking, on bruschetta or in a salad dressing. The oil takes on an intense flavour of the olives and, as a result, is absolutely delicious. Also, no waste!

300 g table salt
2 kg hard, fresh green or black olives
your choice of flavourings: peeled whole garlic cloves, lemon slices, oregano leaves, mint leaves, fennel seeds
extra-virgin olive oil, to cover

Make a brine by bringing the salt and 3 litres of water to the boil in a large stockpot.

Place the olives in clean jars (see steps 1–2, page 21), together with your choice of flavourings.

Pour the still hot brine over the olives, ensuring they are completely submerged but there is still a 2 cm gap at the top of the jars. Seal. As the brine cools, it will seal the jars hermetically to prevent the brine from developing a mould and to keep the olives firm. Store in a cool, dark place for 3 months.

After 3 months, drain the olives and place them in a large glass container, then cover with oil, ensuring the olives are completely submerged. Seal and store in a cool, dark place for 1 month before eating. The olives will keep for up to 2 years unopened. Once opened, store in the fridge, where they will keep for up to 1 month.

Garlic olives

Olive con aglio

1 kg hard, fresh green olives (ideally the giant kalamata variety)
100 g table salt
250 ml white wine vinegar
1 celery stalk, finely chopped
10 flat-leaf parsley sprigs, finely chopped
2 garlic cloves, finely sliced
extra-virgin olive oil, to seal

Cut two slits in each olive and place in a bucket. Cover with water and leave for 7 days, changing the water each day. Finally, drain and set aside while you make the brine.

Make a brine by combining the salt and 1 litre of water in a large stockpot. Bring the brine to boiling point, then allow to cool slightly. Stir through the white wine vinegar while the brine is still hot.

Place approximately two handfuls of olives in a large clean jar (see steps 1–2, page 21), then add some celery, parsley and garlic. Repeat this process until each jar is full. Fill the jars with the still hot vinegar brine, ensuring the olive mixture is completely submerged but there is still a 2 cm gap at the top of the jars. Pour a thin layer of olive oil on top and screw on the lids; the jars will seal hermetically as the liquid cools. Store in a cool, dark place for 3 months before eating. The olives will keep for up to 2 years unopened. Once opened, store in the fridge, where they will keep for up to 1 month.

Variation

Chilli olives
Olive con peperoncino

Follow the same process as the recipe above, except omit the white wine vinegar and make a pickling mixture of one part lemon juice and four parts brine. When adding the flavourings, add chilli powder to taste as well. Allow to sit for 3 months before eating, then store as above.

Toti's crushed olives in brine

Olive schiacciate in salamoia, alla Toti

This recipe is typical of Southern Italy, where the Greek influence can still be found in recipes and the local dialect.

A similar recipe to this suggests crushing the olives at the beach between two rocks. Not particularly practical, but it sounds fun and you would certainly get a lot of interest from passers-by! When I was originally given this recipe by Toti, I was told to use the bottom of an empty beer bottle to crush the olives (this is ideal because the bottom of the bottle is slightly concave so the olives will not launch like scud missiles in all directions). You can also use a meat tenderiser or a rolling pin.

1 kg hard, fresh green olives, pitted and crushed
100 g table salt
1 lemon, sliced
2 garlic cloves, crushed
½ teaspoon fennel seeds

Special equipment
10 litre plastic container

Place the crushed olives in the 10 litre plastic container. Cover with cold, fresh water and allow to stand for 5 days, changing the water twice a day. Drain and set aside while you make the brine.

Make a brine by combining the salt and 1 litre of water in a large stockpot. Bring the brine to boiling point, then allow to cool slightly while you place the olives in large, clean jars (see steps 1–2, page 21), dividing the lemon, garlic and fennel evenly among them as you go. Pour the still hot brine over the olives, ensuring the olives are completely submerged but there is still a 2 cm gap at the top of the jars. Seal. As the brine cools, it will seal the jars hermetically to prevent the brine from developing a mould and to keep the olives firm.

Store in a cool, dark place for 6 weeks before eating. The olives will keep for up to 1 year unopened. Once opened, store in the fridge, where they will keep for up to 1 month.

Squashed olives

Olive schiacciate

This recipe is for freshly pickled green olives. It takes about seven days to prepare and by the eighth day they are all gone! At least in our house they are. Presented here are a number of flavour variations.

Basic recipe
1 kg hard, fresh green olives
50 g table salt
extra-virgin olive oil, to cover

Special equipment
10 litre plastic container

Squash the olives using the base of an empty beer bottle (the indention in the bottom of the bottle will stop the olives flying in all directions). Cover with boiling water for 5 seconds, then drain.

Place the squashed olives in the 10 litre plastic container. Cover with cold, fresh water and allow to stand for 5 days, changing the water twice a day. Taste the olives after 5 days; if they are still bitter, add some sliced lemon to the water and leave for a further 24 hours.

Drain and add the salt and your choice of flavourings. Cover with olive oil and store in the fridge for 3–4 days before eating. They will keep in the fridge for up to 1 month.

Variation 1

garlic cloves, finely sliced
sliced lemon
fennel seeds
dried mint

Variation 2

garlic cloves, finely sliced
dried oregano

Variation 3

garlic cloves, finely sliced
dried oregano
chilli powder
celery, finely chopped
white wine vinegar

Anita's green olives

Le olive della Signora Anita

Select larger green olives (verdale or kalamata) for this recipe. Once you have prepared them with the flavourings, you can place them under olive oil in jars, freeze them, seal them in vacuum bags, or just eat them straight away (I prefer the last suggestion!).

1 kg hard, fresh green olives
100 g table salt
extra-virgin olive oil
2 garlic cloves, finely sliced
1 teaspoon dried oregano
1 teaspoon dried chilli flakes (optional)

Special equipment
10 litre plastic container
10 kg weight (about 4 bricks is ideal)

Place the olives in the 10 litre plastic container. Cover with cold, fresh water and allow to stand for 3 days, replacing the water every day.

After 3 days, drain the olives and crush each one with an empty beer bottle (the indention in the bottom of the bottle will stop the olives flying in all directions). Remove the pits from the crushed olives (ideally have someone else on hand to do this for you!).

Place the pitted olives back in the plastic container and cover with the salt. Cover with a plate or wooden tray, then place a 10 kg weight on top.

Now comes the hard part. Leave the olives in the salt for 3 months, agitating them every 2–3 weeks. You can leave the olives like this for up to 1 year, until you want to use them.

When you want to use the olives, remove them from the brine, place in a sieve or colander and wash quickly under running water to remove as much salt as possible.

Place the olives in a large bowl and add a good splash of olive oil, the garlic, oregano and a little chilli, if you like. Eat straight away or transfer to clean jars (see steps 1–2, page 21) and completely cover with olive oil. Seal and store in a cool, dark place for 1 month before eating. The olives will keep for up to 2 years unopened. Once opened, store in the fridge for up to 1 month.

Variation

As with so many Italian recipes, the ingredients might be the same but it is the person's method that is special! This is Tony Fedele's variation on the above recipe. Tony got in touch with me after I self-published the original version of *Preserving the Italian Way* – it turned out that his father, Pasquale, and my father were both interned as Italian prisoners of war during World War Two, where their job was to cut wood for a local hospital in Warburton, Victoria. Our mothers' villages in Calabria were 10 kilometres apart too. The amazing twists life brings!

For Tony's variation, follow the recipe above but once the olives are under the salt, agitate them every day and they will be ready to use after 14 days.

'I planted five olive trees in the car park of my GP surgery in Melbourne. After patiently waiting for them to mature, I was ready for the first big pick and had organised some friends to help me. But when we turned up on a Saturday morning to reap the fruits of my long wait, they had all been stolen the previous night by some local! The following year, when they were almost ready to pick, to deter the thieves I decided to spray the trees with a bright blue food dye. I placed a sign on the tree saying "Sprayed With Poison, Do Not Eat!" and it worked. When I turned up with my friends to pick the olives, they were all there, like turquoise jewels hanging from Cleopatra's ears. After a thorough wash in fresh water to remove all the food dye, they were ready to pickle. *Il calabrese non è fessa* – the Calabrese is no fool!'

Rosemary's black olives

Olive nere di Rosemary

For this recipe, pick or buy even-sized and firm black olives. Rosemary, a lifelong friend of mine from Northern Italy, says that the manzanillo variety is best.

1 kg hard, fresh black olives
table salt
2 garlic cloves, sliced
1 teaspoon dried oregano

Special equipment
10 litre plastic container

Place the olives in the 10 litre plastic container and cover with cold, fresh water. Leave for 5 days, then drain and cover again with cold, fresh water, measuring how many litres you've used to cover the olives. Add 100 g of table salt for every litre of water to the olives. Mix the salt and olives together and leave for 24 hours, then drain and set aside while you prepare the brine.

Make a fresh salt solution – 100 g of salt for every 1 litre of water – in a large stockpot and bring to the boil. Allow to cool slightly while you place the drained olives in clean jars (see steps 1–2, page 21). Cover the olives with the still hot brine, ensuring they are completely submerged but there is still a 2 cm gap at the top of the jars. Seal immediately. As the brine cools, it will seal the jars hermetically to prevent the brine from developing a mould and to keep the olives firm.

Store in a cool, dark place for 40 days, then strain the brine out of the olive jars, reserving the olives. Make a fresh brine as above and pour the still hot brine over the olives again, before sealing the jars and storing in a cool, dark place for up to 6 months. They will be ready to eat after 3 weeks.

When you want to eat the olives, remove them from the brine and wash with fresh water. Mix through the garlic and oregano, then store the olives in the fridge for 1 day before eating.

Black olives recipe no. 2

Olive nere, ricetta numero 2

1 kg hard, fresh black olives
rosemary sprigs (1 per jar)
dried bay leaves (1 per jar)
lemon peel (couple of strips per jar)
garlic cloves, crushed (½ teaspoon per jar)
100 g table salt
extra-virgin olive oil, to cover (optional)
dried oregano, to taste (optional)
dried chilli flakes, to taste (optional)

Using a sharp knife, cut a slit on either side of each olive. Arrange the olives in clean jars (see steps 1–2, page 21) and add a rosemary sprig, bay leaf, two strips of lemon peel and ½ teaspoon of crushed garlic to each jar.

Combine the salt and 1 litre of water in a large stockpot and bring to the boil. Turn off the heat and allow the mixture to stand for 5 minutes. Pour the still hot brine over the olives, ensuring they are completely submerged but there is still a 2 cm gap at the top of the jars. Screw on the lids; the jars will seal hermetically as the brine cools.

Store the jars in a cool, dark place for 3 weeks. After this time, you can either eat them, leave them as they are until you are ready to eat them (they will keep for up to 6 months), or drain them and place under oil with the oregano and chilli and keep in the fridge for up to 1 month.

My mother's salted black olives

Olive sotto sale, ricetta di mia madre

The olives for this recipe are picked, preferably from your own tree, when the fruit is deep purple and still firm. When handling the olives, be very careful not to bruise or damage them. I find that the best olive varieties for this recipe are picual, verdale or kalamata. Spanish queens do not work as well as they turn out very sweet.

10 kg extra-ripe black olives, with the option
    to cut a few slits in each one before salting
1 kg table salt
4 tablespoons dried oregano
5 garlic cloves, sliced
2 tablespoons fennel flowers or seeds
extra-virgin olive oil, to cover

Special equipment
10 litre plastic container
10 kg weight (about 4 bricks is ideal)

Place the olives in the 10 litre plastic container, cover with the salt and mix well. Cover with a plate or wooden tray and place a 10 kg weight on top. Leave for 5 days, agitating the brine each day.

After 5 days, transfer the olives to a container with holes in the bottom, such as a large colander, and set it over the kitchen or laundry sink. Place the plate or tray and weight on top again and leave for a further 5 days, allowing the brine to drain freely.

After 5 days, depending on the size of the olives, they should be starting to taste sweet and not too salty. To find out, just taste; if they are still too bitter for your palate, leave over the sink for another day or two and continue to agitate.

Once the olives are to your taste, rinse the excess salt off briefly with fresh water, then dry thoroughly (they will be quite shrivelled).

Place the olives on baking trays (there is no need to grease or line them) and dry out briefly in a very low oven (120°C fan-forced) for 10–15 minutes. If the sun is out, they can be dried on trays in the sun for a few hours.

After drying, mix the olives with the oregano, garlic and fennel and place them in clean jars (see steps 1–2, page 21), then completely cover with olive oil. Preserving them this way, they tend to absorb the oil after a period of time and can taste quite heavy.

If you prefer a lighter taste, place them in a container and splash over some olive oil. Store the container in the fridge and occasionally agitate the olives to keep them coated with oil.

My preferred method is to simply place them in a vacuum-sealed bag with approximately 2 tablespoons of oil. Once vacuum sealed, they will keep in the bottom of the fridge for up to 1 year (unless eaten before then!).

Or, once dry, simply bung them in the freezer and defrost them as required, then add oregano, garlic and a little extra-virgin olive oil before serving. Or use them in the delicious fry-up recipe over the page!

Favourite olive fry-up

Olive fritte preferita

There was a doctor in Ferrozzano, a small town in Calabria, who had the following advice for his patients: '*du pipi bruscenti e nu biccher' i vinu sunnu a salutti dell 'omo'*. Translated: two hot chillies and a glass of wine are the health of mankind! My *compare* Vince and I completely agree, and share a love of this fry-up. As well as making an ideal bruschetta topping, you can eat it with pasta (it's pretty much a puttanesca) or dolloped on a bowl of *pasta e fagioli* soup. The spicy and sweet flavours are perfect together!

3–4 tablespoons extra-virgin olive oil
2–3 anchovy fillets
4–5 small Dried Hot Chillies (see page 109), chopped
20 of My Mother's Salted Black Olives (see page 91)
10 capers (preferably small salted capers, rinsed)
3–4 large vine-ripened tomatoes, chopped

In a frying pan, heat the olive oil over medium heat and gently fry the anchovy fillets for 1–2 minutes until they have dissolved into the oil. Add the chilli and briefly sauté. Add the olives, capers and tomato and sauté gently for about 20 minutes or until softened and the tomato juices are reduced.

Enjoy with some homemade crusty bread (*la scarpetta,* the 'small shoe' of bread used to mop up the last bit of sauce on your plate!) and a nice glass of wine.

Ripe Calabrese olives, Greek style

Calabrese olive mature, alla Greca

1 kg ripe black olives
100 g table salt, dissolved in 1 litre water
½ teaspoon dried oregano
3 lemon wedges
2 garlic cloves, finely sliced
375 ml white wine vinegar
extra-virgin olive oil, to seal

Using a very sharp knife, slash each olive deeply on one side to reduce bruising. Place the olives in a large stoneware, earthenware, glass or porcelain container.

In a large stockpot, bring the salty water to boiling point, then pour over the olives to cover. Place a plastic bag filled with water on top of the olives (an old trick!) so that all of them are completely submerged.

Store the olives in a cool, dark place for 3 weeks, changing the brine solution once a week. If a scum forms on the surface during that time, rinse the olives with fresh water before covering with brine again. The scum is harmless, don't worry.

After 3 weeks, taste one of the largest olives. If it is still too bitter, re-brine as above and soak for another week. If the olive you taste is only slightly bitter (they should still have a bit of a tang), pour off the brine and rinse the olives in fresh water.

Place the olives in a clean jar (see steps 1–2, page 21) with the oregano, lemon and garlic, then cover with the vinegar. Finally, pour in enough olive oil to form a 5 mm layer on top of the marinating olives.

The olives will be ready to eat after sitting in the marinade for just a few days. Store, still in the marinade, in a cool, dark place or in the fridge. If kept too long, the lemon and vinegar flavours will predominate so eat these within 1 month.

Paul's olives in brine

Olive in salamoia di Paulo

You will notice that all recipes for olives in brine have two things in common: they use salt and something to acidify the brine, such as lemon juice or vinegar. This is another delicious variation!

10 kg hard, fresh black or green olives, washed in cold water
2 kg table salt
6 garlic cloves, finely sliced (optional)
1 cup fennel fronds, finely sliced, or wild fennel flowers, left whole (optional)
2 tablespoons dried oregano (optional)
500 ml malt vinegar

Place the olives in a large stainless-steel or terracotta container.

Place 10 litres of water and 1 kg of the salt in a large stockpot and bring to the boil, then allow to cool completely.

Pour the cooled brine over the olives, then place a plate or plastic bag filled with water on top to ensure the olives are completely submerged. Leave for 6 weeks, stirring the mixture every 2–3 days. After 6 weeks, taste an olive. They should be sweet or at least have lost their intense bitter flavour. Drain the olives and place them in large, clean jars (see steps 1–2, page 21). You can add garlic, fennel and/or oregano to the olives or just leave them plain.

Make a fresh brine with 10 litres of water and the remaining 1 kg of salt. Stir through the vinegar and bring to the boil. Remove from the heat and pour the hot mixture over the olives, ensuring they are completely submerged but there is still a 2 cm gap at the top of the jars. Seal. As the brine cools, it will seal the jars hermetically to prevent the brine from developing a mould and to keep the olives firm.

Store in a cool, dark place for 4 weeks before eating. The olives will keep for up to 6 months unopened. Once opened, store in the fridge, where they will keep for up to 1 month.

Black olives by Rosa of Cosenza

Olive da Rosa di Cosenza

2 kg ripe black olives
200 g table salt
dried chilli flakes, to taste
extra-virgin olive oil, to cover

Blanch the olives briefly in boiling water, then remove immediately and allow to dry overnight.

Place the olives in a large container and add the salt. Mix well and leave for 1 week, agitating the mixture daily. By the seventh day, they should be sweet. Rinse off the salt briefly and leave the olives uncovered overnight to dry (or if you have a wood-fired oven, place the olives in when the oven is almost cold and leave overnight).

Place the olives in clean jars (see steps 1–2, page 21) with some chilli flakes and completely cover with oil. Seal the jars and store in a cool, dark place for 1 month before eating. They will keep for up to 1 year unopened. Once opened, store in the fridge for up to 1 month.

HERBS AND DRIED PRESERVES

ERBE AROMATICHE E CONSERVE SECCHE

05

On a hot day, if you walk around the average back garden of any self-respecting Italian, you will see racks of tomatoes and capsicums drying on tin roofs. It is the pride of many of my friends and a source of intense competition among them (very un-Italian, don't you think?). This is a very easy and ancient form of preserving that needs just a sustained period of sunshine, constant hot and dry weather and good-quality ripe fruit.

Likewise, herbs are of vital importance in the Italian kitchen. One theory is that because of the lack of refrigeration in the old days, often meat needed to be made edible by adding herbs and spices. I believe that the Italian cook sought inspiration from the garden plot and used every type of herb, whether wild or from the garden, to add flavour, love and excitement to the dishes by stimulating as many senses as possible.

All herbs that are grown in the garden can be dried or preserved in salt or in oil, then used for the rest of the year.

Drying herbs at home

This is an excellent way to preserve your crops of summer herbs to use in the colder months.

You can dry bushy herbs, such as oregano, thyme and rosemary, by tying a bunch of sprigs together, washing them briefly in water and hanging them outside in the sun to dry for up to 10 days.

For herbs that have large, distinct leaves, such as basil or mint, dry the leaves individually on trays outside in the sun. Be careful not to leave them too long as the fragrant oils will also dry out. Three days is usually sufficient.

When the dried herbs are ready, the leaves will easily crumble when rubbed between your hands. You can leave the dried individual basil or mint leaves whole, but you can crumble the bushier ones like oregano and thyme. Place in clean jars (see steps 1–2, page 21) to be used throughout the year.

An alternative, and much quicker, way of drying herbs at home is in the microwave. I actually find that the herbs maintain their colour and aroma better this way than sun-dried. This works well for oregano, sage, thyme, flat-leaf parsley, mint and basil. Simply place the herbs on paper towel and cook on high for about 10–15 minutes. When ready they will be totally dry. Crumble and store in the same way as for sun-dried herbs.

Salted herbs

Erbe sotto sale

The difference between fresh and dried herbs is the amount of natural oils they contain. Dried herbs have only a small fraction of the oils, and therefore flavour, found in fresh herbs. One way to preserve the oils is to salt the herbs when they are still freshly picked from the garden, thereby maintaining the intensity of their flavour.

100 g rosemary leaves
100 g basil leaves
100 g sage leaves
3 garlic cloves, finely chopped
100 g sea salt flakes

Wash and dry the herbs thoroughly, using one of the methods described opposite.

Finely chop the dried herbs and place in a large clean jar (see steps 1–2, page 21) with the garlic and salt, mixing thoroughly to combine.

The herbs are ready to use straight away and will keep for up to 1 year stored in a cool, dark place. Remember that they are salted, so adjust the seasoning in your dish accordingly when using them for cooking.

Variations

Salted basil
Basilico sotto sale

Basil leaves can be preserved whole to maintain their fresh flavour all year round. Simply wash the leaves and pat dry. Place them in a jar with salt flakes between the layers of leaves. Allow to stand. The salt will draw out some liquid, but this is completely fine; just allow the liquid to cover the leaves and add more salt if necessary. The salted basil will keep in the pantry for up to 6 months. Note that when you use this basil in cooking, you probably won't need to add any additional salt to your dish.

Ariosto

This is a dry herb blend used in roasts and stews. The quantities of each herb may vary. Combine dried rosemary, basil, sage, oregano and bay leaves. Add salt and garlic powder to taste, then blitz to a fine powder in a blender. Store in an airtight container in the pantry for up to 1 year.

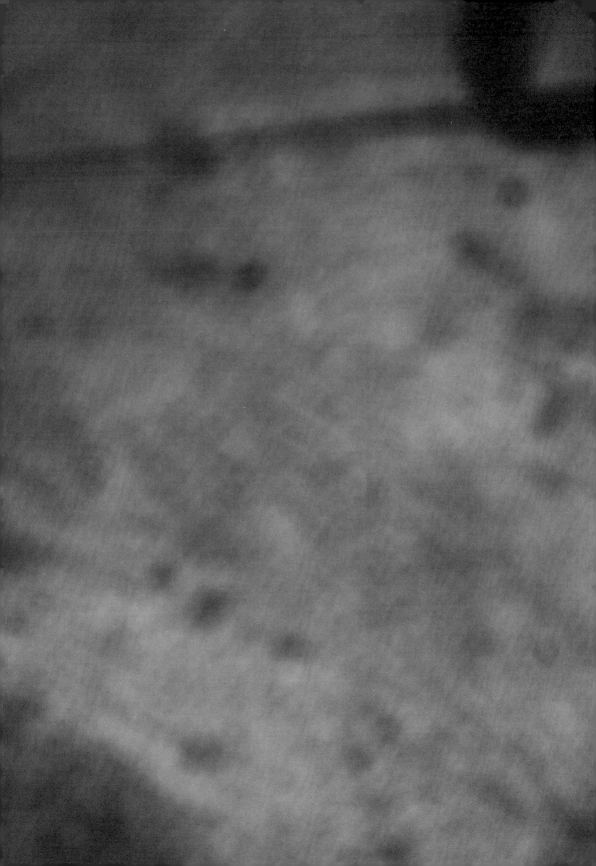

Dried tomatoes

Pomodori secchi

The best tomatoes to dry in the sun are the roma variety, preferably grown in your own garden and picked when the stem is drying up. This guarantees that the tomatoes are actually ripe, rather than sprayed with chemicals to turn red, like the ones you find in supermarkets out of season. To properly dehydrate tomatoes takes two to four hot, dry and ideally windy days.

roma tomatoes, halved
table salt
dried basil or oregano, to taste
garlic cloves, finely sliced (optional)
extra-virgin olive oil, to cover

Place the tomato halves on a wire rack or fine mesh tray (anything where air can easily circulate) and sprinkle with table salt. Place them in full sun (Dad used to put them on the tin roof of the garage). Leave them out all day and make sure you bring them in at night to ensure that they do not collect dew. You then put them out in the sun again the next day! The length of the process varies with the heat and the amount of sunlight, but usually 2–4 days is enough. By this time, the tomatoes should have the consistency of dried apricots, still with a little moisture but obviously dried.

Alternatively, the most convenient way to dry tomatoes (or any other vegetable, such as capsicums), is to buy yourself a dehydrator – it's well worth the investment.

Place the dried tomatoes in a stockpot and add the dried herbs, garlic (if using) and a liberal amount of olive oil. Leave overnight so the tomatoes absorb some of the oil.

The next day, place the dried tomatoes in clean jars (see steps 1–2, page 21) and add more olive oil to completely cover. Seal and store in a cool, dark place for 2 weeks before eating. The tomatoes will keep for up to 1 year unopened. Once opened, store them in the fridge, where they will keep for up to 1 month.

Alternatively, you can vacuum seal the tomatoes after leaving them overnight with the herbs, garlic and olive oil. This means that you don't have to add extra olive oil to cover. Stored like this, they will keep for up to 2 years in the fridge.

Variations

Dried tomatoes with anchovies
Pomodori secchi con acciughe

Dry the tomatoes as opposite. Between each pair of tomato halves, enclose a slice of anchovy, a caper and a thin slice of garlic (and some dried chilli flakes too, if you like). Place the tomatoes in clean jars (see steps 1–2, page 21), layered with some dried bay leaves and oregano. Completely cover with extra-virgin olive oil, then seal and store as opposite.

Dried tomatoes with vinegar
Pomodori secchi con aceto

The tomatoes need to be very dry for this recipe, so if drying them yourself ensure there is no moisture left at all (disregard the note in the original recipe about dried apricots!). Alternatively, commercially produced dried tomatoes are fine to use.

Place the dried tomatoes in a large plastic tub and cover with white wine vinegar. Position a plate or wooden tray on top of the tomatoes, then place a weight (such as four bricks) on top and leave for 24 hours. Remove the weights and drain off the vinegar. Mix the tomatoes with olives – such as Paul's Olives in Brine (see page 93) or My Mother's Salted Black Olives (see page 91) – some capers, finely sliced garlic and dried oregano. Place the tomatoes in clean jars (see steps 1–2, page 21), completely cover with extra-virgin olive oil, seal and store as opposite.

Dried capsicums

Peperoni secchi

red capsicums, cut into 1–2 cm wide strips
table salt
garlic cloves, finely sliced
dried bay leaves
extra-virgin olive oil, to cover

Place the capsicum strips on a wire rack
or fine mesh tray (anything where air can
easily circulate) and lightly sprinkle with table
salt. Place them in the sun to dry as for the
tomatoes (see opposite). Alternatively, use
a dehydrator.

The capsicum strips need to remain slightly
moist and still red, rather than dried to the
stage where they are crisp or brown.

Place the capsicum strips in clean jars
(see steps 1–2, page 21) with some garlic
and one bay leaf per jar. Cover with olive
oil, seal and store in a cool, dark place for
3–4 weeks before eating; they will keep
for up to 6 months. The longer you leave
them, the more vibrant and deep red the
oil becomes; this is delicious to eat with
crusty bread.

Dried prickly pears

Fichi d'india secchi

This is for the true Italophile. I personally
do not go ape over prickly pears, but in
Sicily they are popular in the winter months.
Be very careful when handling prickly pears,
using tongs and thick gloves when picking
and preparing them.

prickly pears, peeled and cut into 5 mm thick
    slices (wear thick gloves when doing this)
table salt

Place the prickly pear slices on a wire rack
or fine mesh tray (anything where air can
easily circulate) and sprinkle lightly with table
salt. Place them in the sun to dry as for the
tomatoes (see opposite) until they become
quite leathery. Alternatively, use a dehydrator.

Store in an airtight container in the pantry
for up to 3 months.

Ciccio's dried figs

Fichi secchi di Ciccio

The best figs for drying are Turkish brown; the small green ones that are golden yellow to amber on the inside. Ideally you would grow them yourself, leaving them on the tree for as long as you can so they become as sweet as possible. But figs are widely available at farmers' markets when in season too.

After picking or buying your figs, place them on a wire rack or fine mesh tray (anything where air can easily circulate) and slightly flatten them. Place them out in the sun every day (bringing them inside at night) and turn them over every second day until they take on a honey colour all over. The whole process takes about 5 days, depending on how constant the sun is! Alternatively, use a dehydrator. Make sure the figs are still slightly firm to press but not moist.

From here there are a number of variations from my mate Ciccio:

Secche al forno

Open up the figs, thread them onto bamboo skewers (which you have pre-soaked in water), then place them in a 120°C (fan-forced) oven for approximately 1 hour or until slightly brown. Allow to cool, then serve. These will keep in an airtight container in the pantry for up to 1 year.

Fichi i padruni

Press several dried figs together to make a ball roughly 10 cm in diameter. Wrap the fig ball in fig leaves and tie up firmly with string. Place in a 120°C (fan-forced) oven for approximately 1 hour. When unwrapped, the figs will be slightly brown and caramelised. They will keep for several months in an airtight container in the pantry.

I crucetti

Cut the dried figs in half without cutting through the stem (so they open up to look a bit like dumbbells). In each half, place an almond or walnut. You can also add a small piece of fresh lemon or orange peel.

Take two of the opened up figs and carefully place the cut surfaces together. Repeat with the remaining figs (so if you had 16 figs, you should now have eight pieces). Arrange the figs on a baking tray so that they cross each other at the stem, forming a crucifix (*i crucetti*). Sprinkle with sugar and place in a 150°C (fan-forced) oven for 30 minutes or until the sugar caramelises. These will last a long time (rather, they *would* keep a long time but they will be eaten quickly!); up to 1 year, so I'm told. When storing, layer them in containers with dried bay leaves and fine slices of orange peel, then sprinkle with sugar and cover with a lid.

Dried hot chillies

Peperoncini secchi

Choose firm, unblemished long red chillies. Using a needle and thread, string the chillies together, passing the needle and thread through their stems. If you pierce the soft flesh, the chillies will rot. Once you have made a long string of them, hang them up in a warm, dry spot, such as the pantry, by your kitchen window or outside in the sun (if you don't live in Melbourne!). You will know when they are dried – they will shrivel up and have no moist skin left. It takes about 10 days.

The dried chillies can be used whole when fried with olives and tomatoes in an abundance of good oil (see Favourite Olive Fry-up, page 92). They can also be pulverised to a coarse powder and used in cooking, in salamis and in all the preserves in this book where dried chilli is called for. The powdered dried chilli can be mixed with extra-virgin olive oil to make a chilli oil, which you can use in *pasta e fagioli* (pasta and beans) or pasta *all'arrabiata* (chilli sauce pasta).

Preserved chestnuts

Castagne sempre fresche

Peel the chestnuts and place them in a container (glass, earthernware or porcelain, not plastic) full of water. Change the water daily, ideally at the same time each day. On the ninth day, drain and place the chestnuts on a tray in the shade to dry. Allow 3–4 days for them to dry completely, then place them in linen bags and store in a cool, dry place for up to 1 year. You now have chestnuts as if they were just picked, all year round!

Grape leaves in vinegar

Foglie d'uva sott'aceto

Pick the grape leaves while they are still young and tender. Wash and dry the leaves.

In a large saucepan, bring some white wine vinegar and salt to taste to the boil. Drop in the grape leaves and boil for a couple of seconds. Remove from the mixture with tongs, drain and then place in clean jars (see steps 1–2, page 21). Always place some extra-virgin olive oil in the jars first to ensure that there are no air pockets. Cover with oil, ensuring the grape leaves are completely submerged, then add some whole black peppercorns. Store in a cool, dark place for up to 1 year. They will be ready to use after 1 month. Once opened, store in the fridge for up to 1 month.

Salted capers

Cappare salate

The Aeolian Islands are famous for producing the best salted capers in the world. When we were on the island of Salina one year, we noticed in the vineyards that at the end of the rows of grapes (they also produce the best Malvasia in existence) they had caper plants rather than roses. I have to say that it made a heap of sense to me because you can't eat roses!

Capers grow well in Western and South Australia. In fact, I received an email from a *paesano* (fellow countryman) in Adelaide who grew capers and wanted to know how to salt them – well, this is how it is done. Ensure you pick the caper flowers while they are still closed. This recipe is from Ernesto from Canneto, Lipari.

1 kg capers
250 g sea salt, plus extra to cover

Place the capers in a non-corrosive container with the salt. Mix thoroughly. Leave for approximately 40 days, mixing daily and draining away any brine that forms. As you remove the brine, add a handful of fresh salt so that the capers are always covered in salt. When you come to bottle them, there should be no brine, just salt and capers. Transfer the capers to clean jars (see steps 1–2, page 21). Seal and store in a cool, dark place for 6 months before using. They will keep for up to 2 years unopened.

Make sure you account for the salt when you cook with these capers, as they are super salty! Alternatively, rinse off the salt under running water before using them in dishes.

'I remember when my wife Lynn and I were visiting a cousin in Florence, and my son Carlo and his girlfriend were stopping with us for a rest during their "European trip". It was a Monday, the day before he was meant to set off again around the rest of Europe, while his girlfriend was catching a plane back to Australia. That evening, there was going to be a railway strike (very common in Europe over the summer) and they needed to be in Rome that night so that his girlfriend could catch her plane the next morning.

But when he woke up that Monday morning, Carlo casually showed me a black mole he had discovered on his back. "That needs to come off," I said after looking at it. I explained the situation to my cousin, that we needed to see a doctor to have the mole attended to. My cousin informed me that GPs in Italy do not remove lesions and that we needed to go to a hospital instead.

"Fine," I said. "Let's go because Carlo needs this off today as he needs to catch the train for Rome tonight."

"Fine," he replied decidedly, "Let's go to the hardware store."

Before I could ask what the hell he was on about, we were driving towards the hardware store, where Carlo's situation was explained to Alberto, the owner.

"Fine," he responded, "I will ring my friend who works in A&E at the hospital and she will see Carlo this morning!"

Feeling very stupid for having doubted my cousin's sanity, we drove off to the local hospital, where we arrived at the emergency department to find the resident already expecting us, as organised. On seeing the mole, she remarked: "That needs to come off."

But ... she did not do procedures and so Carlo would need to see the dermatologist. Well, that's not so bad, I thought. Off to the dermatology outpatients department we went, and at approximately 11 am, we actually got to see the dermatologist.

"That needs to come off," she announced. "But I'm not a proceduralist dermatologist, so I cannot remove it. He will need to see a surgeon. However, the surgeon at this hospital is not available till tomorrow."

I explained that Carlo needed to get the 5 pm train to get to Rome that evening, before the railway strike began. She shrugged. "Sorry, I cannot help you."

By this stage, I was stressing somewhat because I did not want Carlo to be leaving with this potentially dangerous mole on his back while he travelled around Europe for the next month.

"Don't worry," said my cousin. "Let's go to the pharmacist, he will be able to help!"

Bewildered, we then drove to the pharmacist who exclaimed, "I know a great surgeon. I will ring him. Carlo will be able to see him at 4 pm this afternoon."

Mindful that the last train to Rome left at 5 pm, we waited in the surgeon's waiting room till about 4.15 pm, when he called us in and said (yes, you guessed it) "That needs to come off." And then, finally, came the magic words: "I will take it off immediately and give it to you in a jar."

That surgeon was remarkable. Skilled, efficient, neat, and he didn't even charge me as I was a fellow doctor! So, we now had the offending mole in a jar and it was 4:55 pm, with the train scheduled to leave at 5 pm. We were at least 10 minutes away by car.

"Don't worry," said my cousin reassuringly, "trains are always late in Italy since Mussolini was deposed. We will make it." So we drove madly off, breaking every speed limit, and screeched to a halt outside the station at 5.05 pm. Carlo and his girlfriend ran up the steps and miraculously were able to buy their tickets within one minute. And the train? It arrived at 5.10. Right not on time, as expected.

The young ones jumped on board and arrived safely in Rome that night. Carlo's girlfriend left for Melbourne the next day and brought the mole in the jar back to Melbourne. She delivered it to my surgery to be sent to pathology for histology.

It turned out to be benign.

Recalling this story reminds me of why I love being in Italy so much. It is the feeling of not being surprised at anything. Somehow, out of total chaos and madness, everything turns out well. Just like making a sauce.'

SAUCES AND SYRUPS

SALSE E SCIROPPI

06

In Italy, everything involving food was, and often still is, an excuse for a *festa* (celebration). There is always a lot of preparation, often several days' work and plenty of opportunity to taste the fruits of your labour – whether it is the preserving of *tonno* (tuna), making cheese and ricotta, or salamis, or grappa – with a multitude of helpers and friends. Making sauces, particularly *pomodoro* (tomato), is no exception.

Tomato sauce–making day begins with the collection and cleaning of carefully emptied beer bottles (another excuse for a party). The crown-seal caps are bought, often in advance otherwise the deli tends to run out of them, and the machine to separate the tomato skins and seeds from the pulp is at the ready. At this stage, you have your first cup of coffee with *biscotti di casa* (homemade biscuits) and a glass of grappa. Then, the fun starts!

Tomato sauce / purée / concentrate / passata

Purè e concentrato di pomodoro

Making tomato sauce or passata is an essential part of the year in an Italian household. Tomatoes form the basis for many, many meals, and most Italians have no concept of restraint so will plant far more than the average household needs.

As a family, we use approximately a hundred 750 ml bottles of passata per year. That is about 100 kg of tomatoes. The making of the sauce is a fun day where everyone from grandmothers to children can participate – from cleaning bottles to chopping tomatoes to pouring the sauce into jars and sealing them. Usually by the end of the day there is tomato juice everywhere and the children are covered in juice and seeds.

There are several ways to make the sauce – some easier than others. The term *passata* refers to tomato sauce that has been passed through a machine, with the skin and seeds removed. To do this easily, if the tomatoes are firm, they need to be heated or boiled – although with an electric machine the raw tomatoes can be passed through as is. If you use a machine, make sure you pass the pulp through two or three times to extract as much of the juice as you can.

Whatever process you use, make sure that the tomatoes you are going to preserve are the best you can get – ideally, genuine vine-ripened roma tomatoes from your own garden or that of a friend. I am sure everyone has a *compare* who grows them! Modern, chemically ripened supermarket tomatoes are low in sugar and high in acid. This increases their shelf life but doesn't give you the sweet flavour of a sun-ripened tomato.Check your tomatoes for ripeness by cutting them open. Even if they're red on the outside, they may be greenish or pale on the inside – a sign of chemically ripened tomatoes, which are no good for this recipe.

There are basically three ways that you can make passata by machine:

Uncooked

Pass the raw tomatoes through the sauce-separating machine and bottle the tomato sauce as is. You can add basil and chilli if you like (though some people feel adding basil at this stage makes it bitter – up to you), then seal with crown seals and sterilise as described opposite.

Cook then seal

Boil the tomatoes in large quantities in a large cauldron for about 20 minutes. Drain in a large colander for several hours, then pass the tomatoes through the sauce-separating machine. Bottle the sauce (with the option to add basil, onion or chilli) and then seal with crown seals. Sterilise as described opposite. This produces a much more concentrated sauce.

Cook then drain

Boil the tomatoes in large quantities in a large cauldron for about 20 minutes, then tip onto a clean muslin sheet and allow to drain for up to 24 hours. This will allow a certain amount of clear liquid to drain, leaving a dense paste.

The paste is then passed through the sauce-separating machine and bottled. The bottles are then sealed and sterilised as described opposite. This produces a sauce that is lower in acid and very tasty, but obviously not in the same volume as the first or second methods.

Always leave approximately 2 cm from the top of the bottle and crown seal securely (if the bottles are overfilled, they will explode during the sterilising process). Once sealed, sterilise as below.

If you make more than 40 bottles – and what self-respecting Italian would make less than 100? – they can be sterilised by boiling them in a cauldron or 44-gallon drum (which will hold approximately 110 bottles).

The drum is placed on a tripod, or above the ground so that a fire can be lit under it. The first layer in the drum needs to be approximately eight to ten layers of newspaper. The bottles are then placed on their sides in layers, with sheets of newspaper between each layer to stop the bottles bumping against each other as they boil (this will lead to broken bottles). Top everything with a layer of multiple sheets of newspaper. Finally, the drum is filled with water. A fire is then lit under the drum, and the drum contents slowly brought to the boil and left boiling for at least 2 hours. The bottles are then left to cool overnight.

But be very careful! If the sterilisation is incomplete, the sauce will ferment and the bottles will explode. Incomplete sterilisation may also produce botulism, a very dangerous form of food poisoning.

This reminds me of the first time I made this tomato sauce with my wife (then girlfriend) Lynn. I was out to impress her with my knowledge of traditional Italian cooking. Unfortunately, I did not have a large enough drum to sterilise the bottles so we left them with a trusted friend to boil. The next morning, after picking them up, we placed the bottles carefully and lovingly in the kitchen cupboard. It turned out that he had not boiled the sauce bottles for long enough, because a week later Lynn was woken up by multiple loud explosions. Every one of the bottles exploded, spreading a foul-smelling 'red peril' all over the kitchen. It took many days to clear the small kitchen of the mess and smell, and some years to convince her to make the sauce again, and that I knew what I was doing.

Store the sealed bottles in a cool, dark place for up to 3 years. The sauce is ready to use straight away; once opened, store in the fridge for up to 1 week.

Variation (the easiest way!)

My preferred method is the easiest way! I bottle the tomatoes without cooking or using a machine. This allows me to keep *all* of the tomato and juice. It also means that all I need are the tomatoes, bottles or jars with lids and the boiling pot – no special equipment and only one process. I use clean (see steps 1–2, page 21) wide-mouthed bottles, such as juice bottles, or large pickle jars. If you want to make sauce the traditional way – 100 bottles at a time – then use crown-seal bottles.

Halve or quarter the tomatoes and place them in the bottles or jars. Roughly crush the tomato with the handle of a wooden spoon until the containers are filled to about 2 cm below the rim, then wipe the rims and seal. Place a clean towel in the bottom of a large stockpot and place the bottles or jars on top. This stops them from rattling and breaking.

Fill the stockpot with water to approximately 2 cm beneath the rim of the lids. Slowly bring the water to boiling point over a 40 minute period. This is very important, as you want the centre of the bottle or jar to be the same temperature as the outside. Once you reach boiling point after 40 minutes, turn the heat down and simmer for at least 40 minutes, then turn off the heat and let the bottles or jars cool in the stockpot overnight.

Once the tomatoes have cooled, you'll often have 4–5 cm of clear liquid at the top of the bottles or jars. Do not throw this away – it is pure tomato juice and full of flavour.

Check that the centres of the lids are firm and drawn inwards. If any lids have popped out, it means that container has not sealed, so you will need to use the produce immediately or repeat the above process using a different lid.

Obviously, the sauce will contain tomato seeds and skins. If you prefer a smooth sauce, pass it through a mouli or simply blitz it in a food processor.

Store the sauce as described opposite. When using it for pasta, cook the pasta in the sauce for the last 2–3 minutes so that it soaks up any excess liquid.

Capsicum paste

Salsa di peperoni

Around April or May, when capsicums are at their reddest and cheapest and becoming a little dry, buy a box at your greengrocer or market to make this excellent paste of many uses, the preferred one being for Calabrese Salami (see page 189).

red capsicums, washed, dried and cut into
    2–3 cm wide strips

Place the capsicum strips in a large saucepan with about 125 ml of water; just enough to stop the capsicum strips from sticking while they cook.

Cook over a low heat for approximately 2 hours or until most of the excess fluid has evaporated.

Pass the capsicum through a sauce-separating machine or a mouli, then, following the instructions on page 21, spoon the paste into clean bottles or jars, leaving a 2 cm gap at the top of the bottles or jars. Screw on the lids and seal hermetically in a hot water bath for 20 minutes to ensure they are airtight.

Store in a cool, dark place for up to 2 years, though it can be eaten straight away. Once opened, store in the fridge for up to 1 month.

Another way to preserve the paste is to spoon it into wide-rimmed jars and cover with a layer of salt, roughly 1 cm thick. If using this method, make sure you allow for the extra saltiness when using the paste in a recipe, particularly for the salami.

Variation

Hot chilli paste
Peperoncini piccanti

Instead of capsicums, use a box of long red chillies. Prepare in the same way as the capsicum paste but make sure that you wash your hands thoroughly after handling the chopped chillies, especially before going to the toilet. If you don't, you will soon discover for yourself why I suggest this!

Pesto, Genovese style

Pesto alla Genovese

35 basil leaves, washed and dried
30 pine nuts
2 large garlic cloves, peeled
250 ml extra-virgin olive oil,
    plus extra to seal
50 g pecorino, grated
pinch of salt

Simply place all the ingredients in a blender and blitz until you have a fine paste. Following the instructions on page 21, spoon the paste into a clean jar and cover with a thin layer of olive oil, leaving a 2 cm gap at the top of the jar. Screw on the lid and seal hermetically in a hot water bath for 30 minutes to ensure the jar is airtight. Store in a cool, dark place for up to 1 year. Once opened, store in the fridge for up to 2 weeks.

Variation

Aunt Nannina's recipe
Ricetta della Zia Nannina

Make the pesto as above but with only one garlic clove, 100 g of pecorino and a small bunch of flat-leaf parsley added.

I sciroppi

Summer is a magical time in Italy. Long, hot days, a series of celebrations and festivals, and multiple trips to the mountains or beaches. Syrups are a fantastic way to enjoy the flavours of summer all year round. You can add them to cakes, milk or your morning porridge, or use them to make gelato or granita. Such wonderful memories!

Raspberry syrup

Sciroppo di lamponi

2 kg raspberries
2.3 kg sugar
juice of 2 lemons

Roughly puree the raspberries with a hand-held blender, then add the sugar and lemon juice and combine.

Bring the mixture to the boil in a saucepan and boil for 3 minutes. Allow to cool slightly, then, following the instructions on page 21, siphon into clean bottles, leaving a 2 cm gap at the top. Screw the lids on and hermetically seal the bottles in a hot water bath for 20 minutes to ensure they are airtight.

The syrup will keep for up to 1 year stored in a cool, dark place. Once opened, store in the fridge for up to 6 months.

Lemon syrup

Sciroppo di limone

When preparing the lemons for this recipe, peel them first – carefully, to avoid too much of the white pith, which will make your syrup bitter – and then juice.

600 ml freshly squeezed lemon juice
650 g sugar
peel of 2 lemons, cut into long strips

Strain the lemon juice into a saucepan. Add the sugar and strips of lemon peel and heat slowly until the peel is transparent. Discard the peel.

Following the instructions on page 21, siphon into a clean bottle, leaving a 2 cm gap at the top. Screw the lid on and hermetically seal the bottle in a hot water bath for 20 minutes to ensure it is airtight.

The syrup will keep for up to 1 year stored in a cool, dark place. Once opened, store in the fridge for up to 6 months. This syrup can be added to water to make a wonderfully refreshing summer drink.

Mint syrup

Sciroppo di menta

1.5 kg mint leaves
peel and juice of 1 lemon
450 g sugar

Wash the mint leaves and pass through
a mouli, finely chop in a food processor or,
if you have neither piece of equipment, chop
finely using a sharp knife. Place the mint in
a large bowl, mix through the lemon peel
and juice, and leave for 2 hours to infuse.

In a saucepan, combine the sugar with 100 ml
of water and bring to the boil. Allow to cool,
then add the mint and lemon mixture. Strain
the syrup into a jug, then pour carefully into
a clean bottle (see steps 1–2, page 21). Seal
and store the syrup in the fridge, where
it will keep for up to 6 months.

Pomegranate syrup

Sciroppo di pomegranate

2 kg pomegranates
approximately 4 kg sugar

Cut the pomegranates in half and squeeze
out the seeds and juice by hand into a large
bowl or saucepan. Discard any small, hard
seeds that are not easily squeezed out –
these are bitter.

Leave the juice and seeds to stand for
24 hours, then strain through a clean muslin
bag into a large stockpot (which you have
weighed first). Discard the seeds.

Once you have strained all the pomegranate
juice into the stockpot, weigh it, subtract
the original weight of the stockpot, and then
add double that amount of sugar to the
pomegranate juice. For example, if your
net weight of pomegranate juice is 1.8 kg,
you need to add 3.6 kg of sugar.

Bring to the boil and simmer for 20 minutes
or until it is thick and has a deep red colour.

Remove from the heat and allow to cool,
then siphon the syrup into a clean bottle (see
steps 1–2, page 21). It will keep for up to 1 year
in a cool, dark place. Once opened, store
in the fridge for up to 6 months.

Perfumed syrup

Sciroppo profumato

This is a delicious syrup that can be used to flavour gelato or granita, or used as a topping for cakes, porridge or cereal. The cherries need to be the amarena variety as they add a tartness to the syrup.

1.4 kg amarena cherries, pitted and
    stems removed
1 kg redcurrants, stems removed
600 g raspberries
peel and juice of 1 lemon
2.8 kg sugar

Place the cherries, redcurrants and raspberries in a large container. Add the lemon peel and mix well. Cover with a plate or wooden tray (but no need for weights this time) and leave the fruit to macerate for 2 days.

After 2 days, use a fine sieve or a clean muslin bag to strain the juice into a large stockpot. Add the lemon juice and sugar and gently bring to the boil. Allow the mixture to boil for 4 minutes, stirring constantly. Remove from the heat and allow to cool briefly.

Following the instructions on page 21, siphon into clean bottles, leaving a 2 cm gap at the top. Screw the lids on and hermetically seal the bottles in a hot water bath for 20 minutes to ensure they are airtight.

The syrup will keep for up to 1 year stored in a cool, dark place. Once opened, store in the fridge for up to 6 months.

Redcurrant syrup

Sciroppo di ribes

You will need 1.2 kg of sugar for every 1 litre of redcurrant juice. The quantity of redcurrants below should produce roughly that amount.

2 kg redcurrants, stems removed
1.2 kg sugar

Place the redcurrants in a large container, crushing them with your hands. Cover and leave for 3–4 days to macerate.

After 3–4 days, strain the juice through a clean muslin bag into a stockpot and add the sugar. Bring to the boil and allow to boil for 10 minutes, stirring constantly. Remove from the heat and allow to cool briefly.

Following the instructions on page 21, siphon into clean bottles, leaving a 2 cm gap at the top. Screw the lids on and hermetically seal the bottles in a hot water bath for 20 minutes to ensure they are airtight.

The syrup will keep for up to 1 year stored in a cool, dark place. Once opened, store in the fridge for up to 6 months.

Blackberry syrup

Sciroppo di more

1.5 kg blackberries, wiped clean (but preferably
    not washed)
1.4 kg sugar
peel and juice of 1 lemon

Place the blackberries in a large bowl or dish,
squashing and squeezing them with your
hands. Cover and leave for 24 hours.

The next day, place the crushed berries
in a large saucepan with the sugar and lemon
peel and juice. Mix well until the sugar has
almost dissolved into the crushed berries
and lemon juice. Bring the mixture to the boil
and allow to boil for 2 minutes. Remove from
the heat and allow to cool briefly.

Following the instructions on page 21, siphon
into a clean bottle, leaving a 2 cm gap at the
top. Screw the lid on and hermetically seal
the bottle in a hot water bath for 20 minutes
to ensure it is airtight.

The syrup will keep for up to 1 year stored
in a cool, dark place. Once opened, store
in the fridge for up to 6 months.

Quince paste

Cotognata

This sweet preserve, as you may know,
is simply excellent with sharp cheeses,
particularly a stunning blue.

2 lemons
1 kg quinces, peeled and cut into 2 cm pieces
1 kg sugar

Zest one of the lemons and juice both.
Place the quince in a large stockpot and
add the sugar, lemon zest and juice. Slowly
bring the mixture to the boil, then simmer
over a very low heat, stirring constantly, until
it is the consistency of polenta. This can take
up to 1½ hours.

Pour the mixture onto a greased and foil-
lined 28 cm x 18 cm baking tray and allow
to cool. Once cool, cut into small squares and
store in an airtight container, with baking
paper between layers. It will keep for up
to 1 year in the fridge.

BREAD

PANE

07

To the Italian, bread is the basis on which all meals are built. In times of need, it was truly the sustenance that kept families going. In my mother's case, it was particularly important.

In 1937, 12 years before I was born, my father left Varapodio for Australia, with the intention to stay and work for two or three years and then return to his village. My grandfather had done this before him, going to New York City in search of work in 1906. The meagre wage he was paid in America was a small fortune in Italy at the time. It allowed him to buy a small stone cottage back home (about 5,000 lira at the time) and help his sons with a dowry of 1,000 lira each when they got married. My dad had similar plans for his own family. When he left, at the age of 31, he and Mum (who was 29) already had four children under six years of age and she was newly pregnant with another. So some more money would be very useful!

After a six-week boat trip, he landed at Port Melbourne. No one was at the pier to meet him. Dad was illiterate and did not understand a word of English. However, at the time, in Peel Street (which is next to where the Queen Victoria Market is today) there was an Italian family who provided temporary lodging to the steady flow of Italian men who were coming to Australia in search of work opportunities. After two days, Dad was on his way to Swan Hill by train, hoping that his cousin would be at the station to meet him. He was. For two years, Dad worked out there and my parents communicated through letters that were written down and read for them by relatives and friends.

But in 1939, the war totally severed any possibility of communication between Mum and Dad. For five years, neither of them knew whether the other was alive or dead. Dad had no idea what had happened to his family, whether he would ever see any of them again. But they believed in each other and knew that they would be reunited.

In her later years, my mother became a fairly dependent and fragile lady, dressed in mourning black – it was hard to believe she was the same woman from Varapodio who worked picking olives, hoeing ancient unforgiving soil for up to 14 hours a day, and raised a young family on her own for more than 10 years. With Dad gone and no way to get money to us, everyone needed to contribute to the income of the family. My eldest brother, once he turned six, had a herd of pigs and goats to attend to. My eight-year-old sister was sent to *la maestra* (a teacher) to learn how to sew and became the seamstress for the household. The rest of the family took their turn working in the field picking olives in the winter, and beans, corn and broad beans in the summer and autumn. Spring was for hoeing and tilling the soil.

Just before the war broke out in 1939, Mum had managed to buy a small house in town for 12,000 lira. And by small, I mean three by six metres. This was to house Mum, my three sisters, two brothers, the sheep, the donkey and the large trunk that contained all of Mum's worldly possessions (*u casciune*). In 1942, when the war was raging with no end in sight, Mum realised she could not continue to raise a family without some kind of enterprise. So she built a small oven under her window, and under the oven she kept three sows and a boar.

After working in the fields hoeing and collecting olives during the day, Mum would collect small branches and sticks to bring home for the oven at night, where she would make bread. At that time, any kind of grain or legume would be ground to make bread: chickpeas, broad beans, dried beans, corn, chestnuts and even acorns. These were ground by hand at night and the resulting flour was made into bread. She usually started baking around 11 pm, working well into the early morning. Once the bread was made, she would collect the ashes from the oven and these would be used on the *braciere*. This was a brass plate placed under the table or *circio*, which would keep the family warm during the damp and cold winters.

The next day she would sell the loaves and she would receive 30 lira, or one egg, or 500 grams of salt, for each loaf of bread. Towards the end of the war, she would sometimes walk 30 kilometres a day into the mountains to collect wood for her bread oven, bringing back close to 100 kilograms of it on her head.

My older sister told me that while food was so scarce during the war and all the other families in the village lived on wild grasses and beans, or whatever they could scrounge, we as a family never went without bread, thanks to Mum.

In 1948, my mother and her five children left Varapodio to join her husband in Australia. They were on one of the first plane loads of women and children to come to Australia from Italy, and the plane journey took six days! They were greeted on arrival by my father, who, despite being a prisoner of war for five years, had been able to buy his first farm in Swan Hill. The day after Mum arrived she had already joined Dad in planting tomatoes and peas. Once in Australia, they never looked back and never went hungry again. Dad built a wood-fired oven for the family and then proceeded to build a new oven in each of the five homes we occupied over the next 40-odd years.

It is hard to believe that in one generation, that kind of poverty became a thing of the past for my family. Thankfully, my parents were reunited. My own children now live lives of unlimited opportunities and want for nothing, thanks to the courage of my parents and their unquenchable desire to give their children everything they didn't have.

Bread making

Bread making is a huge subject on which hundreds of books have been written. I am going to talk about the basic bread that my mother, and others like her, made – the huge *pagnocchi* (a round loaf with a hole in the middle). This type of bread is still made in Italy today, though it is perhaps not as well known as focaccia or ciabatta. *Pagnocchi* is a crusty, tasty bread with an aroma and texture that is even better the next day. It can also be used when stale as the basis for panzanella, a Florentine bread and tomato salad.

To make bread, it goes without saying that you will need an oven. If you want to make truly authentic Italian bread (or 20 kilograms of bread at once), why not give building your own wood-fired oven a go?

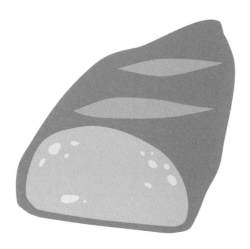

Building a wood-fired brick oven

For an approximately 1 metre diameter oven you will need:

a base for the oven (this can constructed from concrete, brick, stone, metal
    or timber – I have given an example below, but have a look online for
    something that suits your taste and budget)
approximately 600 kg sand (enough to fill 0.4 m^2)
approximately 190 full bricks (ideally firebricks but standard red clay is fine)
1 × 60 cm stick
approximately 335 half bricks (ideally firebricks but standard red clay is fine)
3 × 10 kg bags of fireproof and waterproof mortar mix
chipboard (for oven door template)
1 × 14 cm diameter oven flue (approximately 90 cm long)
1 × bluestone keystone
a small piece of plywood
2 pads of 'pink batts' insulation
2 fireproof tiles (for oven door)

You can use ordinary red clay bricks for your oven, but I suggest using proper
firebricks, which heat up quickly and easily withstand the high temperatures
needed. You can also make your own mud bricks to build the oven (for instructions
on how to make those, consult an appropriate manual or look online).

    First, you will need a base on which to build your oven, bearing in mind
that the finished oven should sit at standard bench height (90 cm). Your base
can be as simple or elaborate as you like and made from whatever materials suit
your taste and budget. I suggest preparing a section of ground approximately
2 m square. On the ground, make a concrete pad approximately 15 cm thick.
This will form the foundation for the oven and the floor of the wood-storage area.
On top of the slab, build a 70 cm high three-sided box (using bricks or blocks)
in the shape of an 'E' (FIG. 1, page 138). Place a sheet of 10 mm thick cement
sheeting on top of the bricks (FIG. 2, page 138). This forms the base of the area
where the oven is to be built.

    You then form a layer of sand approximately 10 cm thick (FIG. 2, page 138)
on top of the cement sheeting. This acts as a base and also insulates the oven
against loss of heat through the bottom. Place a layer of firebricks on the bed of
sand approximately 1.8 m by 1.8 m (FIG. 2, page 138), which will be about 180 full
bricks (you'll use about 10 more for the oven door opening).

    The inside of the oven will be approximately 1.2 m in diameter. The opening
at the front will be approximately 45 cm wide and approximately 30 cm deep
(or one full brick and one half brick). Using a stick 60 cm in length, place one end

of the stick at the centre of the oven. You use the opposite end as a guide to lay the first row of half bricks (FIG. 3, page 138).

As there will be a larger gap on the outside of the bricks than along the inner oven face, you will need to use a reasonable amount of mortar to fill in the gaps. Try to have as little mortar as possible on the inside surface so that it is mainly a brick face (FIG. 4, page 138).

Using the stick as an inside guide, continue laying the half bricks in a circular fashion, locking in with the oven door (FIGS 5 and 6, page 138). You will probably find that you can only lay four to five rows each day in order to allow the bricks to set, before laying the next lot.

To make the oven door, it is easier to use a chipboard template the shape of the door, to act as a guide and support for the laying of the bricks (FIG. 7, page 139). As you get to the top of the door and the oven dome, insert a 14 cm diameter flue approximately 90 cm long to allow the smoke to escape, and hold in position (FIG. 8, page 139).

You will need a keystone at the top of the opening to finish the entrance (FIG. 9, page 139). The last two to three rows of half bricks in the dome need to be laid one row at a time. To prevent the bricks from falling, lay a piece of plywood up against the dome and then lay the bricks on the plywood, using the stick as support (FIG. 10, page 139). Leave this in place for at least two days to allow the mortar to dry. You could also use a flat pliable surface to support the last bricks. Bolster the surface with some support from some pliable 3-ply, a box or a stick, and lay the last rows of bricks directly on the ply (FIG. 10, page 139).

Once the oven is finished, you will have a smooth surface on the inside and the cut or broken brick surfaces facing outwards. You then cover the outside of the oven with the pink insulation batts: these will help insulate the oven and prevent heat loss. Finally, render the outside of the batts with a fireproof and heatproof mortar mix. You can also add colouring to the mortar, or you can attach decorative elements like shells or mosaics. Make sure that you secure the flue to a wall or verandah.

If you wish to have the oven under cover, once you have finished the process above, continue the walls of the footings (FIG. 11, page 139) to encase the whole oven. Fill the enclosure with sand (FIG. 12, page 139). This acts as insulation for the oven but is not essential. Place a roof over the lot, preferably with nice terracotta roof tiles. Lastly, make a door with a fireproof tile for the inside and outside of the mouth of the oven. The inside door will seal the oven during cooking.

Variation

Follow the instructions above, up to where you begin building the walls of the oven. At this point, you need to build a frame or form the shape of the inside of the oven. This can be made out of wood or built up sand. Once you have made the shape, you simply cover the form with the bricks.

When the mortar has dried, you either set fire to the wooden frame or dig out the sand from inside the finished oven. The final steps are the same as in the instructions above.

Using the oven

Before using the oven, allow it to dry thoroughly for a week, then try lighting a couple of very small fires. This ensures that the walls are totally dry before you light your first real fire, and it will prevent cracking. You are now ready to make bread!

First, you need to stoke up the oven. This is done using sticks and dry wood that will burn readily, as well as larger pieces to generate a high temperature. Initially, the oven lining turns from black (due to the smoke) to a pale grey and then to white as it heats up and the smoke particles burn. Once the inside of the oven is an even white, the oven is ready. At this point, sweep the ashes to one side using a cotton mop that has been soaked in water and thoroughly wrung dry. Wipe this over the base and sweep the surface you plan to cook on completely free of ashes. This is to ensure that the baking area is clean and that you will not end up with charcoal or ashes on the base of your bread or pizzas. Allow the oven to rest for five minutes after cleaning.

To test the heat of the oven, either use a thermometer or throw some flour onto the hot base of the oven. The flour should gradually turn a golden colour within a few seconds and not burn. If it burns as you watch, it means that the oven is too hot. If this is the case, just leave it for 15 minutes, or clean the base again with the mop and repeat the procedure with the flour. The oven is now ready.

Your bread dough (page 142) that has been kneaded and twice risen is now ready to be placed into the oven using a well-floured wooden or metal spatula. Close the door (or mouth) of the oven and seal with wet rags around the outside of the door to prevent heat from escaping. Leave the oven and the bread alone for at least 20 minutes.

Once you get used to your oven you will know when your bread is ready, but after around 20 minutes the oven can usually be opened. At this point, be ready to be absolutely overwhelmed by the incredible aroma of fresh bread, which will send your senses into overdrive. It will remind you that the world truly is a beautiful place and once experienced (and I hope all children are lucky enough to experience this in their childhood), the aroma of bread fresh from the oven will be a trigger for hundreds of memories.

When ready, the bread will be a lovely golden brown and it will sound hollow when you tap the base. At this point, you can either eat it fresh or dehydrate it for *biscotto* or *pane secco* (page 143).

And of course, warm bread fresh from the oven is just crying out for a good olive oil and sun-dried olives, to be enjoyed with a glass of wine!

Naturally, your new wood-fired oven can and will be used for more than just bread making. It can be used to cook roasted meats with potatoes and rosemary, a range of pizzas and lasagne to die for! Because this oven lets you cook for a crowd, I recommend inviting 30–40 of your friends over to try it out.

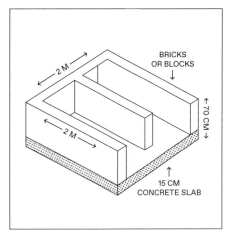

FIG. 1

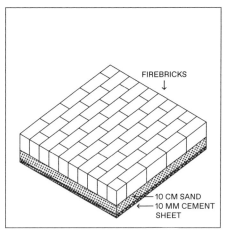

FIG. 2

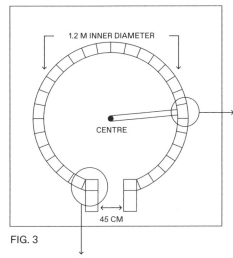

FIG. 3

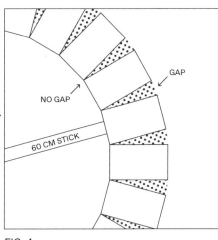

FIG. 4

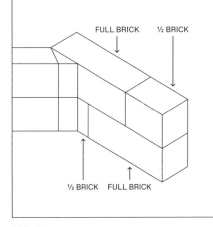

FIG. 5

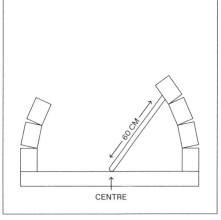

FIG. 6

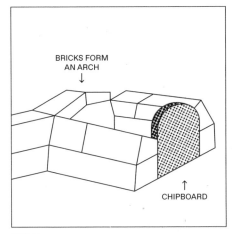

FIG. 7

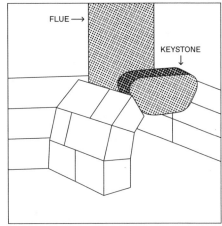

FIG. 8

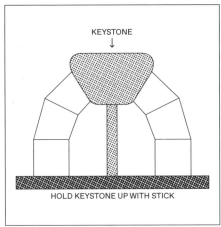

FIG. 9

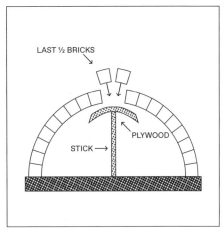

FIG. 10

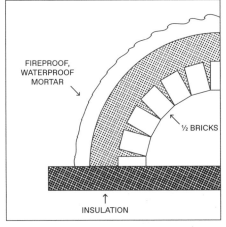

FIG. 11

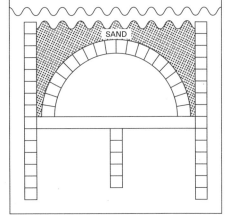

FIG. 12

Pane

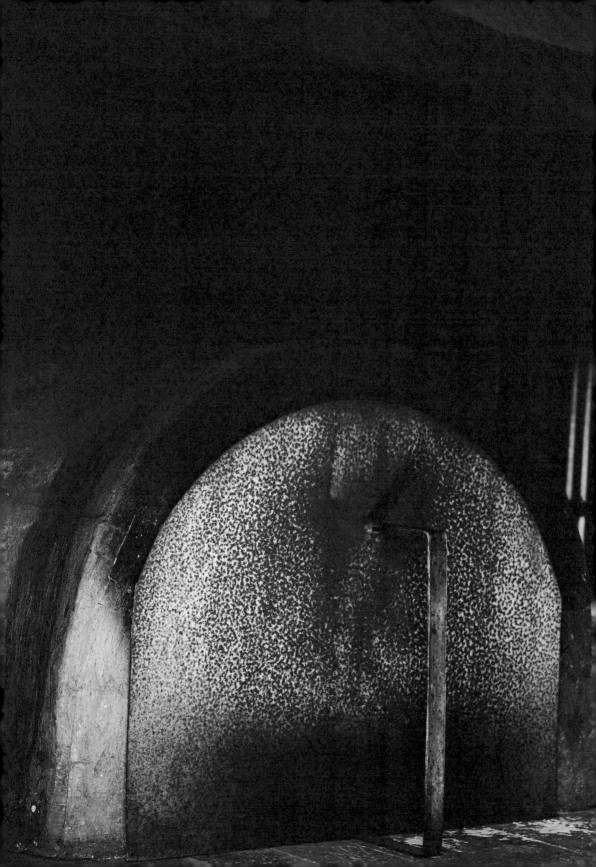

Country bread

Pane di campagna

This is the basic recipe for making bread simply with plain, unbleached flour (whether you buy it in bags from the supermarket or grind your own, as my mother would have!), water, salt and baker's yeast, which you can buy from any supermarket. The rest is hard work and lots of practice to get it right. But it's great fun – and delicious!

Makes 2 medium loaves

1 kg plain unbleached flour
1 teaspoon dried yeast dissolved
    in 3 tablespoons warm water,
    set aside for 10 minutes
750 ml lukewarm water
20 g salt

Place the flour on a clean work surface and form a well in the centre. Slowly add the yeast mixture and the water to the centre of the flour, then sprinkle in the salt. Now begin to mix it all together with your hands. Once the water and flour are combined, continue kneading for approximately 20 minutes or until the dough loses its stickiness and is soft and velvety. Kneading bread is great for stress management, so I'm told!

Place the dough in a large container (make sure there's plenty of room for it to expand) in a warm spot and cover with a damp tea towel. Allow to rise until the dough has tripled in size (which will take approximately 3 hours).

Flour your work surface well and tip the dough out. Cut the dough in half and flatten each piece. Rotate and stretch the dough out several times. It should feel springy, soft and pliable. Finally, shape your two loaves into mounds, tucking the ends in neatly (or not, if you prefer a more rustic look!). Cover again with the damp tea towel and leave on the bench for another hour or until the loaves have doubled in size.

At this point, if you do not have a wood-fired oven, preheat your oven to 230°C fan-forced. I like to place a terracotta tile in the oven as it heats up, on which to bake the bread – this is the closest you can get to recreating a wood-fired oven. If you do have a wood-fired oven, follow the instructions for preheating and preparing it on page 137.

When your oven, wood-fired or otherwise, is ready, place the loaves inside. Follow the instructions on page 137 if you have a wood-fired oven. For a regular oven, allow the loaves to bake for 50–60 minutes or until they are golden brown. Remove from the oven and tap the bottoms. There should be a hollow sound, indicating that the loaves are cooked through. Place on a wire rack to cool.

Variations

Herb bread
Pane con erbe

You can add all sorts of extras to the dough at the end of the kneading process. Try various herbs, such as rosemary, for a classic *pane con erbe*, or add pitted black olives, small cubes of mozzarella or even some *peicchi* (pre-fried pork skin).

Bread with endive
Pane con cicoria

Make the dough as opposite. While waiting for the first rise, cook some endive – or any greens, such as escarole (*scarola*), English spinach or even silverbeet leaves – in boiling water, then drain and cool. Place a frying pan over medium heat and add some good-quality extra-virgin olive oil, the greens, pitted salted black olives and two or three anchovies. Cook for a few minutes until everything is well combined and the anchovies have 'melted'. Allow to cool.

Flour your work surface well and tip the dough out. Cut the dough in half and flatten each piece. Rotate and stretch the dough out several times. It should feel springy, soft and pliable. Stretch the dough out a final time and place half of the endive mixture in the middle of each piece. Fold the dough over and shape into two loaves, then follow the proving and cooking instructions opposite.

Dried bread
Pane biscotto or *pane secco*

Remove your bread from the oven and, while still hot, split the loaves into two or three sections. Place these pieces back in the oven. If using a wood-fired oven, seal the oven door and leave overnight in the residual heat. If using a regular oven, turn the temperature down to 100°C and leave overnight. The next day, the bread will be completely dried out – when you remove it, it will literally shatter in your hands. Store it in an airtight container in the pantry, where it will keep for months.

This dried bread is absolutely fantastic for an antipasto. Break it into large pieces with your hands and quickly pass them under running water, then shake off the excess. Place the slightly moistened dried bread on a plate and top with a drizzle of extra-virgin olive oil, chopped fresh tomatoes from the garden, salt and dried oregano. This is truly delicious.

Sourdough ciabatta

Ciabatta casalinga

The basic fact about all home preserving is that it needs to be simple and use as few ingredients as possible. My mother did not have elaborate equipment or a long list of added ingredients when she made her bread. This is a modern take on her recipe that I now like to use.

The actual time spent preparing this bread is less than 15 minutes, then it's just a matter of setting it aside to ferment and prove. The longer you leave the *biga* (starter) in the fridge, the more of a pronounced sourdough flavour you will achieve.

500 g bread flour, plus extra for dusting
½ teaspoon dried yeast
1 tablespoon table salt
1 tablespoon extra-virgin olive oil

To make the *biga* (starter), combine 200 g of the flour, the yeast and 200 ml of water in a large bowl, then place in the fridge for 12–24 hours.

Remove the *biga* from the fridge, then add the remaining 300 g of flour, the salt, olive oil and 160 ml of water. Mix well, cover with a tea towel and set aside to prove in a warm spot for 3 hours. Every 45 minutes, turn the dough over from four even points around the bowl, then cover and return to the warm spot. You will do this four times.

Preheat the oven to 240°C fan-forced. As soon as you turn the oven on, fill a tray with water and place it in the base of the oven (this will heat up and create steam when cooking the bread; essential for a lovely crusty loaf!). Line another baking tray with baking paper and dust liberally with flour.

Gently turn out the dough onto the prepared tray, being very careful not to knock the air out of it. Flour the dough liberally, cut it into two pieces, then very gently shape these into loaves. Allow the dough to rise for another 35 minutes while the oven heats to 240°C.

When the dough is risen and the oven fully heated, slide the tray of bread into the oven. You will get a blast of steam when you open the oven door – this is what you want!

Cook the bread for 12 minutes, then rotate the tray and cook for a further 12 minutes.

Allow to cool on a wire rack, then eat with a drizzle of extra-virgin olive oil, some *Melanzane Sott'olio* (see page 29) or fresh butter and homemade jam.

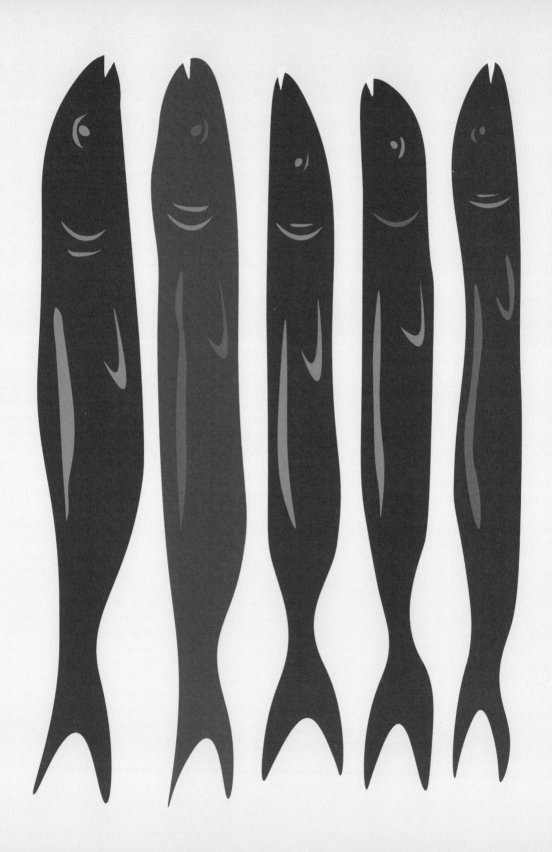

FISH

PESCE

08

'Iddu va e iddu veni colla piscia ente la manu ...'
('Where are you going, where are you coming from, carrying a fish in your hand ...')
– From the Sicilian folk song 'O Mamma, mi svoju maritaa'.

Italians have always had a special love for the sea and the vast array of food that it has to offer. Every Mediterranean table knows the sharp taste of a sardine eaten with a piece of crusty bread, or the sweet flavour of tuna or mackerel with fresh tomatoes and basil, or even *risotto al tonno* (tuna risotto).

My friend Mimmo, who was born in Erculaneum (the original city buried by the eruption of Vesuvius in 79 CE), remembers when his grandfather, a fisherman, would return after being at sea for several months. He would usually arrive late at night, with a large tuna draped in a sheet over his shoulder. The flurry of activity that followed saw the whole household getting up to help with the cutting, boiling and bottling that took place late into the night. Well lubricated with good wine, I so enjoy sharing these stories of great catches and singing *stornelli* (traditional sea shanties). Sure beats just going to the deli for a can of tuna!

Like vegetables, fish can be preserved in several ways: *sotto sale* (in salt), *sott'olio* (in oil), *salamoia* (in brine) and *sott'aceto* (in vinegar). You will find examples of all of these methods throughout this chapter.

Sardines in salt

Sardine sotto sale

There are many sardine recipes from different regions of Italy, but they all have one thing in common – they stink the kitchen out when you prepare them, but everyone loves to eat them when they are ready! This is a great recipe to make while on holiday at the beach – hence some of the instructions.

Always buy sardines (or *alici,* which are smaller and without scales) as fresh as possible. You can tell if the fish is fresh by checking that it is firm and stiff, and that the eyes are full and clear. While we're on that subject, my friend Mimmo once told me about the 'eye painters of Napoli' in his town, Erculaneum (just south of Naples), whose job was to paint fish eyes black to make old fish look fresh. I'm sure your local Australian fishmonger does not engage in such practices, but still … it always pays to check!

This quantity of sardines will fill a 2 litre glass jar. These can be eaten on their own with fresh bread and a glass of good white wine, or you can fillet them and use them instead of anchovies to make a wonderful *pasta alla puttanesca.*

4 kg fresh sardines
3 kg rock salt
6 garlic cloves, finely sliced
15 g dried oregano
dried chilli flakes (optional)
extra-virgin olive oil, to cover

Special equipment
10 litre plastic tub or bucket
10 kg weight (about 4 bricks is ideal)

Place the sardines in the 10 litre plastic tub or bucket. Mix in about 1 kg of the rock salt, finishing with a layer of salt on top. Make sure that every fish is covered in salt but be gentle when you mix them or you will damage the fish. Leave the sardines in a cool place, uncovered, for 24 hours.

The next day, take the sardines – still in the tub or bucket of salt – to the beach. Wash the excess salt off with sea water, removing all the blood and any loose scales. When at home again, remove the heads and entrails with a sharp knife. Do not try to remove the scales at this stage as you'll damage the fish.

Place the sardines in a stoneware or stainless-steel pot, layering with the remaining rock salt and finishing with a thick layer of salt. Cover with a plate or circular piece of wood, then place a 10 kg weight on top.

Leave the sardines in a cool, dark place to cure in the salt for at least 28 days and up to 40 days. Every person I've spoken to leaves them for a different amount of time – one allows the sardines to remain under salt for up to 2 years before eating!

Remove the weights and wash the salt off the fish using a 50:50 solution of fresh water and white wine vinegar. At this point, you can remove any remaining scales. Dry the sardines thoroughly.

Place the sardines in a large clean jar (see steps 1–2, page 21), top to tail. Add the garlic, oregano and chilli flakes (if using). Before you cover with oil, drain any excess brine out of the bottom of the jar, which may have collected during this process.

Finally, cover with good-quality olive oil, ensuring the sardines are completely submerged. Seal and leave for up to 4 weeks in a cool, dark place before eating. Once opened, keep the sardines in the fridge, where they will keep for up to 1 week.

Variation

Pilchards with chilli
Alici al peperoncino

Instead of sardines, you can use pilchards. These are slightly smaller than sardines and do not have any scales. Follow the same recipe as above and just add a generous amount of chilli when placing in the jar with the oil.

Salted anchovies

Acciughi sotto sale

This recipe comes from Cetara, the centre of the anchovy (*acciughe*) world, where the very best specimens come from.

Of course, here in Australia there are different fish and different values placed on them. In Australia, the *Engraulis australis* or Australian anchovy is not commonly sold for human consumption but mostly for bait. It is very rare that you will see fresh ones for sale. So you can make this recipe with smaller fresh sardines, as they have a similarly strong taste.

1 kg small fresh sardines or pilchards, washed, heads and entrails removed
table salt
white wine vinegar, to soak
extra-virgin olive oil, to serve
garlic cloves, finely sliced, to serve
fresh or dried oregano, to serve

Special equipment
large, wide-mouthed ceramic jar
wooden disc (the same size as the opening of the ceramic jar)
5 kg weight (about 2 bricks is ideal)

Place the cleaned fish, top to tail, in the ceramic jar, sprinkling salt in layers with the fish, ensuring each one is covered in salt, until the jar is full. Finish with a 100 g layer of salt.

Place the wooden disc on top of the salted fish, then place the 5 kg weight on top and leave for 3–4 months until the fish take on a pink/orange tinge (don't be alarmed, this is normal!).

When you want to eat them, remove the fish from the jar, rinse them in fresh water, then soak in white wine vinegar for 1 minute. This helps to balance the saltiness.

Drain the fish, remove the bone from the fillets, lay out on a plate and serve with a drizzle of extra-virgin olive oil, some garlic and oregano.

Marinated sardines

Sarde marinate

This couldn't be simpler. Use only the freshest sardines you can find. If you can find fresh pilchards, they work well here too.

1 kg sardines, cleaned, with heads, entrails and spines removed
200 ml white wine vinegar
extra-virgin olive oil, chopped flat-leaf parsley and lemon slices, to serve

Place the fish on a deep plate in layers and add the white wine vinegar. Leave for 4 hours.

Remove the fish and pat dry with paper towel. They will be a white/grey colour because the proteins have been 'cooked' by the vinegar.

Arrange the fish on a plate and serve with extra-virgin olive oil, chopped parsley and (if you really want to impress your partner) a slice of lemon, as it looks very nice!

The sardines will keep for up to 1 week in the fridge and are very appetising as part of an antipasto spread.

Variation

In lemon juice
In spremuta di limone

Use lemon juice instead of vinegar to 'cook' the fish. This is a popular way to do it in Naples! Follow the recipe above but instead of vinegar, cover the fish in fresh lemon juice and a sprinkle of salt. Leave for 24 hours in the fridge. When the flesh becomes a pearly grey colour, the fish is 'cooked' and ready to eat. To serve, drizzle with olive oil and sprinkle over some chopped flat-leaf parsley.

Whitebait with salt and hot chilli

Bianchetti piccanti sotto sale

In Australia, any tiny fish that can be eaten whole are referred to as 'whitebait', though apart from an unrelated species called Tasmanian whitebait, there isn't an official 'whitebait' in Australia, nor a commercial fishery for them.

1 kg whitebait (*neonata*)
250 g table salt
chilli powder, to taste
fennel seeds, to taste
extra-virgin olive oil, to cover

Special equipment
10 litre plastic container
5 kg weight (about 2 bricks is ideal)

Place the whitebait in the 10 litre plastic container and cover with the salt. Place a plate or wooden tray on top, followed by a 5 kg weight. Leave to stand for 1 month.

When ready, remove the weights and transfer the whitebait to a chopping board. Combine with the chilli powder, fennel seeds and a generous splash of olive oil, kneading as though you are making bread, until everything is well combined.

Transfer the whitebait to clean jars (see steps 1–2, page 21) and press down so that the oil floats to the top and the whitebait is completely submerged. Top up with more oil if necessary, then seal. Store in a cool, dark place for up to 1 year. The fish can be eaten after 1 month; once opened, store in the fridge for up to 1 week. The whitebait can be used as a base for pasta sauces, such as *aglio olio* and *acciughi con pepperoncino*.

Sardines in oil

Sarde sott'olio

2 kg fresh sardines, cleaned, with heads, entrails and scales removed
table salt
dried bay leaves
whole black peppercorns
extra-virgin olive oil, to cover

Place the sardines on a chopping board and set the board on an angle, with one end in the sink or a container to catch the juices as they drain off. Cover the fish with salt and allow to drain for 3 hours, then turn them over and cover with salt again. Leave for a further 2 hours.

When ready, rinse off the salt and pat the fish dry with paper towel.

Place the sardines in clean jars (see steps 1–2, page 21) and layer a couple of bay leaves and some whole black peppercorns through each jar. Allow to stand for 1 hour, then completely cover with olive oil, leaving a 2 cm gap at the top of the jars. Screw on the lids.

Hermetically seal the jars (see page 21) in a hot water bath for 1 hour to ensure they are airtight. Store the sealed jars in a cool, dark place for up to 1 year. The sardines can be eaten after 2 weeks; once opened, store in the fridge for up to 1 week.

Sardines in saor

Sarde in saor

This recipe is from the Veneto/Trevisano region. *Saor* is a milder version of *carpione* (*saor* is the contraction of *savor*, which in Venetian dialect means 'flavour'), which is basically a sauce made with fried onions and vinegar. It is used to marinate fresh fish, especially sole and sardines. Other variations include pine nuts, raisins and sugar.

5 kg fresh sardines, cleaned, with head, entrails and scales removed, butterflied (get your fishmonger to do this)
plain flour, for dusting
extra-virgin olive oil
table salt
6 red onions, sliced
750 ml white wine vinegar

Wash and dry the sardines, then roll them in the flour.

Heat a splash of olive oil in a large frying pan over medium–high heat and fry the sardines for 10 minutes or until both sides are golden brown. Drain on paper towel and salt liberally, then set aside.

In the same pan, heat some more olive oil over medium heat. Fry the onion, adding a sprinkle of salt to draw out the moisture (this ensures the onion doesn't stick to the pan). Reduce the heat to low, cover and cook for 10–15 minutes or until the onion is soft and caramelised. Try not to add water, as you will be adding the vinegar shortly.

When the onion is cooked, add the vinegar, stir well and remove the pan from the heat. Allow to cool.

In a large glass dish, layer the sardines and cover each layer with the vinegar and onion mixture. Repeat until you have used everything up, then cover and place in the fridge, where the sardines will be ready to eat after 2 days. They will keep in the fridge for up to 2 months, but are best eaten within 1 month.

Marinated pilchards

Licioccole marinate

This preserve is great to serve as part of a seafood antipasto.

white wine vinegar
table salt
1 kg very small pilchards, washed in salt water, heads and entrails removed
garlic cloves, finely chopped
dried oregano
dried chilli flakes
extra-virgin olive oil, to cover

Make a solution of six parts white wine vinegar and one part water. Add salt to taste, as if you were preparing to cook pasta. Marinate the fish in the solution for 48 hours, then remove and allow to drain overnight on a clean towel.

The next day, mix the fish in a bowl with your desired amount of finely chopped garlic, oregano and chilli, plus a splash of olive oil.

Pour a splash of olive oil into a clean jar (see steps 1–2, page 21), then fill with the fish. Repeat with as many jars as you need. Cover with oil, ensuring the fish are completely submerged, then seal and store in a cool, dark place for up to 1 year. The fish can be eaten after 1 month; once opened, store in the fridge for up to 1 week.

When serving, add some extra finely chopped garlic and olive oil.

Nonna Iacono's tuna in oil

Tonno sott'olio della Nonna Iacono

When I think of this recipe, I go back to Sant'Angelo on the isle of Ischia. It is a balmy spring evening in 1996 and we are on the balcony of Il Pescatore, the restaurant owned by our dear friend Assunta Iacono. Looking out on the marina full of small colourful fishing boats, the sun setting bright red over the 'Torre', a small peninsula winding round in front of the piazza, embracing the fishing boats and protecting them from harm like a loving mother. My children are eating their frappé and I am sitting, writing down recipes from Nonna Iacono and sipping a *limoncino* (see page 247). At that moment, who cares if we never go back home!

Nonna was a restaurateur all her life and the matriarch of the Iacono family. She was amazing in her youthful attitude, and intensely interested in us as a family and as Italians from a far-off country.

You will need a very fresh and very large tuna for this. If you can, fish one out of the Pacific Ocean or Great Australian Bight yourself! The best varieties are the albacore (*Thunnus alalunga*) or yellowfin (*Thunnus albacares*).

Otherwise, go to a fish market and choose a good-sized fresh tuna. I love going to a fish market – it's fantastic seeing so much fresh fish at incredibly good prices. The hard thing is getting it home in the car. Take at least one friend, maybe two or three, with you if you're buying a 50 kg tuna.

Once, when making this recipe in Italy with my friend Mimmo, we went to the fish market early in the morning to pick up a tuna. The fishmonger gave us an enormous polystyrene box with the tuna on ice. It looked like a coffin! And so, out of the market and into the mists of the early morning Mimmo and I emerged, carrying the tuna in its coffin and laying it reverently on the back seat of the car. We got a lot of stares! The only thing missing was the *Godfather* theme!

50 kg fresh albacore or yellowfin tuna, cleaned and gutted, cut into 10 cm thick slices
5 kg table salt
light olive oil, to cover
garlic cloves, finely sliced
lemons, sliced
dried bay leaves
small red chillies (optional)

Special equipment
large cauldron
wide-necked preserving jars

Place the tuna slices and salt in the large cauldron. Cover with water. Simmer for 3 hours over low heat. This is best done on a barbecue or over a fire outside, as otherwise your house will be filled with a cooked tuna smell that lingers around for days, even weeks!

Drain the cooked tuna slices and place on clean tea towels. Leave overnight to cool.

The next morning (before your partner gets up and realises that the sink is covered in large slabs of tuna and the kitchen smells of fish!), remove the skin and bones from the tuna.

Pour a splash of olive oil into clean, wide-necked jars (see steps 1–2, page 21), then divide the pieces of tuna among them, packing down firmly. Add some garlic, lemon slices and bay leaves to each jar. If you like it hot, you can also add a small chilli to each jar. Completely cover with a good-quality light olive oil, leaving a 2 cm gap at the top of the jars. Screw on the lids and hermetically seal the jars (see page 21) in a hot water bath for at least 2 hours.

Store in a cool, dark place for at least 1 month before eating. The tuna will then keep for up to 1 year unopened. Once opened, store in the fridge for up to 1 week.

Once you have eaten all the tuna, use the leftover oil to make an unforgettable risotto!

Variations

Mackerel in oil
Sgombri sott'olio

Mackerel has a much stronger taste than tuna but can be prepared in exactly the same way. Follow the recipe opposite, with 120 g of salt for every 1 kg of fish.

Tuna in brine
Tonno in salamoia

Prepare the fish as opposite, but instead of oil, use a fresh brine made with 60 g of salt for every 1 litre of water. Place the fish and flavourings in clean jars (see steps 1–2, page 21), then completely cover with the brine, leaving a 2 cm gap at the top of the jars. Seal hermetically (see page 21) in a hot water bath for at least 2 hours, then store as opposite.

Bonito in oil
Bonito sott'olio

Bonito are smaller 4–5 kg tuna that are easily found at fish markets. Follow Nonna Iacono's recipe opposite, using 100 g of salt for every 1 kg of fish. After boiling the fish and removing the skin and bones, place the fish in clean jars (see steps 1–2, page 21) with garlic, dried bay leaves and chilli to taste. Completely cover in oil, leaving a 2 cm gap at the top of the jars. Screw on the lids and hermetically seal the jars (see page 21) in a hot water bath for at least 2 hours. Store as opposite.

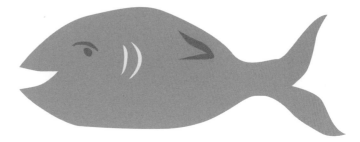

Fruits of the sea (seafood)

Frutti di mare

Use whatever combination of seafood you like for this recipe, depending on what you have available at the time. Below is a particularly good mixture.

1 litre white wine vinegar
table salt, to taste
2 kg mixed seafood (I recommend baby octopus, cleaned; legs of larger octopus, cleaned; mussels, shelled; pipis, shelled; small prawns, shelled and deveined)
extra-virgin olive oil, to cover

In a large stockpot, combine the white wine vinegar with 1 litre of water and add salt to taste (approximately 1 teaspoon per 1 litre of liquid). Bring to the boil.

Carefully add the seafood, then reduce to a simmer and cook for 30 minutes. Drain and leave the seafood on a clean tea towel on the bench to cool overnight.

The next morning, follow the instructions on page 21 and place the seafood mixture in clean jars. Cover with oil, ensuring the seafood is completely submerged but there is still a 2 cm gap at the top of the jars. Screw on the lids and hermetically seal the jars in a hot water bath for at least 1 hour to ensure they are airtight.

Store in a cool, dark place for up to 6 months, but the seafood is ready to be eaten straight away. Once opened, store in the fridge for up to 1 week.

Baby octopus, squid or calamari in vinegar

Polpo, sepie o calamari sott'aceto

1 litre white wine vinegar
1 carrot, sliced
1 onion, sliced
1 celery stalk, including leaves, sliced
table salt, to taste
3 kg baby octopus, squid or calamari, cleaned
1 garlic clove, finely sliced
lemon slices (optional)
1 dried bay leaf
2 tablespoons pitted green olives
10 whole black peppercorns

In a large stockpot, combine 2 litres of water with 250 ml of the white wine vinegar, the carrot, onion, celery and salt to taste. Bring to the boil. Add the octopus, squid or calamari and cook for 10 minutes. Remove from the heat, drain and allow to cool before placing the seafood and vegetables in clean jars (see steps 1–2, page 21) with the garlic and some lemon slices, if you like.

In another stockpot or large saucepan, boil the remaining vinegar with the bay leaf, olives and peppercorns for 10 minutes.

Completely cover the octopus, squid or calamari with the hot vinegar mixture, leaving a 2 cm gap at the top of the jars. Allow to cool before screwing on the lids and hermetically sealing the jars (see page 21) in a hot water bath for at least 1 hour to ensure they are airtight.

Store in a cool, dark place for up to 6 months, but the seafood is ready to be eaten straight away. Once opened, store in the fridge for up to 1 week.

Calabrian caviar

Rosamarina sott'olio

We recently travelled back to my parents' village to catch up with my cousins. What food, what weather and what a welcome! Once we left Varapodio, we travelled a short distance to Gioia Tauro, a seaside port city.

As my wife Lynn and I were walking along the *lungomare* (promenade), we saw about 20 people all running and converging to one spot on the beach. Of course, being a doctor, I immediately assumed someone had had a cardiac arrest so I sprinted forward, shouting, 'Out of the way, I am a doctor … let me through!'

To my surprise, instead of some poor fellow convulsing on the sand, I found a woman selling the very first whitebait of the season. Well, after trying to explain my bizarre behaviour, I began talking to the fisherwoman about one of the best *rosamarina* (whitebait) recipes, known as Calabrian caviar.

And guess what? She had the best recipe, so here it is.

1.5 kg whitebait (*neonata*), washed in salt water
250 g table salt
500 ml white wine vinegar
100 g chilli powder (ideally Dried Hot Chillies crushed to a powder, see page 109)
extra-virgin olive oil

Special equipment
large plastic tub or bucket
5 kg weight (about 2 bricks is ideal)

Mix the whitebait with the salt in the large plastic tub or bucket. Place a plate or wooden tray on top, followed by a 5 kg weight. Leave for 7 days, agitating the mixture thoroughly each day.

When ready, rinse the fish with the vinegar and lay out to dry outside on a clean tea towel. Once dry, sprinkle over the powdered chilli and mix thoroughly with your hands (wearing gloves), ensuring all the fish are coated in the chilli.

Mix the fish with some olive oil and place in clean jars (see steps 1–2, page 21). Cover in more oil, ensuring the fish are completely submerged. Store in a cool, dark place for 1 month before eating. The fish will keep for up to 1 year unopened. Once opened, store in the fridge for up to 1 week. Enjoy on crusty, toasted bread with a glass of crisp pinot grigio alongside.

Variation

There are many recipes for Calabrian caviar, all involving salt and chilli with oil, but the quantities vary to be more or less hot or salty. Whichever way you make it, it is a memorable eating experience!

To make a less salty version with a few different flavours, follow the recipe above but use only 175 g of salt and add the chilli powder and 100 g of ground paprika to the initial mixture with the salt, which you leave for 4 days instead of 7 days. Place a sprig of wild fennel in the jars before sealing and storing as above.

Salt-cured tuna

Tonno salato

Before fridges and freezers, it must have been very difficult to keep fish fresh. Can you imagine a fisherman coming home with a 50–60 kg tuna on his shoulders and there being no cool place to store it? The solution was to salt it.

This recipe produces a tasty but very salty tuna meat. It is traditionally thinly sliced and eaten with bread as an antipasto, or used in cooking like anchovies.

50 kg bluefin or yellowfin tuna, cut into
    4 cm thick slices
approximately 6 kg table salt
white wine vinegar
extra-virgin olive oil, to serve

Special equipment
large non-corrosive vat or container
10 kg weight (about 4 bricks is ideal)

Place the tuna slices in the vat or container, adding 40–60 g (up to two fistfuls) of salt between the layers of fish. Keep repeating the process until all the fish is under salt. Cover with a plate or wooden tray and place the 10 kg weight on top.

Store this in the fridge and leave for up to 1 month until you are ready to eat it. It will reduce to approximately 50 per cent of the original volume.

To serve, remove the number of tuna pieces you want and rinse off the salt with white wine vinegar. This will reduce the saltiness. Serve thinly sliced with a drizzle of olive oil.

Salted fish roe

Bottarga

When we visited our friend Ciccio in Cavriglia in 2000, we were served a very delicate pasta with a slightly salty fish flavour. This was my introduction to bottarga. The most famous example of this dish is made from mullet eggs from Orbitello, a lagoon in Tuscany. It is also made with tuna roe, but here in Australia I have used any fish roe, ranging from mullet and ocean perch (this is a beautiful deep orange) to flathead and snapper, and I think they are all equally good. The important thing is that the fish roe is very fresh. If it has an off smell, don't buy it!

Bottarga has a beautiful flavour and is lovely served on a thin slice of crusty bread with a good olive oil (not too strong, maybe a mature picked Frantoio). It is also excellent grated over a simple pasta of *aglio e olio* just before serving – fantastic!

undamaged fish roe or egg sacks, from
    extra-fresh fish (ideally mullet)
sea salt (approximately 30 g per egg sack)
olive oil, for brushing

Place the roe in a small container and cover in sea salt for 2 hours.

Brush off the excess salt and hang the roe to dry out in the fridge, where it is cool and ventilated. Make sure you put a plate underneath the roe to catch any liquid. Allow to dry for approximately 7–14 days or until the roe is firm but still with a bit of give.

Brush the dried roe with oil, wrap in plastic wrap and store in the fridge until it becomes too dry to grate over your pasta! Alternatively, seal it in a vacuum bag and store in the fridge for up to 1 year.

CHEESE

I FORMAGGI

09

'*Ricotta frisca!*' (fresh ricotta!). I can still hear the *massaro* (shepherd) calling out under our balcony at my uncle's house in Varapodio. My aunt went down to buy small, delectable portions of fresh ricotta made with sheep's milk, sold in tiny handwoven reed baskets. The ricotta was still warm.

Enchanted by the flavour and freshness of the cheese, the next day I went to meet the shepherd at his hut or *baracca* made of old branches and reeds. Sheep were grazing and bleating nearby and a large cauldron of milk was heating over an open wood fire. The whole area was hazy with smoke and the wafting smell of sheep and fermenting milk. I felt like I had wandered into a scene from history, going right back to Ancient Greece!

The shepherd added to his cauldron of milk a small piece of (vegetarians, look away) salted kid (baby goat) stomach that he fetched out of a smelly jar, and miraculously the milk began to curdle. We sat around the cauldron, ready with fresh bread and deep plates into which he ladled the fresh ricotta and whey. It was sublime. I wondered how many generations of young Italians this delicate junket had nourished.

Almost all my friends have a relative who used to be a *massaro* in Italy, and therefore made their own cheese. There are so many ways to make it. A *compare* of mine comes from Ferrozzano near Locri in Calabria. He and his wife now live in the suburbs of Melbourne, where they make the most wonderful cheese that you can either eat fresh with crusty bread and a glass of homemade red wine, or cure to grate onto pasta or other dishes. My *compare* makes the cheese in his laundry in the back garden and stores the cured, dried forms in his garage, ready to be shared with friends and family.

It fascinates me how at the basis of every traditional recipe there is a very strong scientific reason as to why it works. Our ancestors may not have realised what contribution the weather or season made, or why it was essential to place products in particular caves or in certain containers; all they knew was that they had been doing it for centuries and followed the instructions faithfully.

Of course, when you try to transplant that process to another country on the other side of the world, where the weather, raw materials and knowledge are very different, this can lead to disasters and disappointments because we simply cannot recreate the process as our families would back home.

I have spent some time with Paul Vitale, whose father was a *massaro* in Ragusa, Sicily, for more than 30 years. When Paul came to Australia, he had many failures using his father's traditional cheese-making techniques. Paul took numerous cheese-making courses to help him understand the process behind the 'old ways', so he could try and reproduce cheeses that resembled those in Italy. He has now been doing this on his dairy farm in Gippsland for 30 years. Of course, the cheeses will never be exactly the same – the cows are different, the pastures are different, the seasons are different, the ingredients are different, even the bacteria in the vats are different, and all of these things have a specific and dramatic effect on the taste and texture of the final product. Paul kindly reviewed the recipes included here. As I have attempted to do throughout this book, I have tried to make the traditional 'word of mouth' recipes and information accessible. But it was also important that they were reviewed by someone who has more knowledge than I do, to give us an understanding of the process and some finer points in the technique. So *grazie*, Paul!

Making your own cheese is more technical than the other home preserves in this book, but it is certainly achievable. The milk can be from a cow, goat or sheep, or you can use a mixture as desired. The sale of raw, unpasteurised milk is banned in Australia, so unless you have access to your own cow, goat or sheep you will have to make do with what is available. But the good news is that there are some excellent non-homogenised, full-cream organic milks available, even at the supermarket. I am going to give instructions assuming you are legally able to get fresh milk from somewhere, but you can still make good cheese, particularly ricotta, using commercially available pasteurised milk (see pages 171 and 176).

Rennet (or another curding agent) is an essential ingredient in cheese making. A number of curding agents have been used in the past. The most common of these is the rennet found in the lining of an unweaned kid or calf stomach. The animal is slaughtered before it is weaned, and its stomach preserved in salt. You can try this yourself but I must warn you that your partner and children are likely to leave home! You can also buy pure rennet in a bottle from your pharmacist or local cheese supplier.

There are also a number of vegetarian rennets used in cheese making. A traditional Italian one is the flowers of the artichoke or Scotch thistle. When these are in bloom, cut them in half, tease the stamens out and mix them with a little warm water. A few drops of the resulting black juice will curdle milk. In Tuscany, they use this rennet for their famous pecorino cheese. My *compare* tells me that when he was a child in Italy, helping to look after the family's flock of sheep from the age of six, they would leave home every morning with only some bread for lunch and a small saucepan. When they were hungry, they would milk a sheep, warm the milk in the saucepan over a fire, collect some thistle flowers, crush the stamens and squeeze the juice into the warm milk. The milk would curdle, making a fresh cottage cheese to be eaten with the bread.

When making ricotta, the sap from a fig stem can be used to curdle the milk. This is done by cutting the stem of a fig branch four or five times. (Be very careful when working with fig sap as it can irritate or burn the skin.) Heat the milk in a saucepan and as it comes to the boil, stir the milk with the cut fig branch so that the sap from the stem mixes with the milk. This will cause the milk to curdle and form ricotta. Some people say that this produces more ricotta! However, if you stir it for too long it is too *riscaldante* (warming) and will cause diarrhoea if too much is eaten (at least, this is the belief in Italy). So the easiest, most sociable and most reliable way to curdle milk without using animal rennet is to use junket tablets.

Cheese

Formaggi

This recipe will make three large cheeses and about 14 *ricotte*. The cheese will vary in taste and fat depending on the time of the year and the diet of the animals. The best time to make cheese in Australia is in spring, from September to November. At this time of year, the milk has just the right fat level. Cheese that is low in fat will produce a harder, sharper cheese that is more suitable for grating. A higher-fat cheese will be softer and less sharp, so more suitable to be eaten fresh.

60 litres fresh unpasteurised milk (cow, goat, sheep or a combination)
1 dessertspoon rennet
500 g table salt

Special equipment
large stainless-steel stockpot or cauldron
thermometer
3 × 1 kg cheese baskets (you can buy plastic ones or get them made from reeds by a basketmaker)
14 × 250 g ricotta baskets (I use small butter or margarine containers with about 20 holes made in the bottom and sides)

Firstly, put aside 4 litres of the milk, which you will use to make ricotta (see page 170).

Pour the rest of the milk into the large stainless-steel stockpot or cauldron and heat to 36°C, stirring constantly and slowly. Once it reaches that temperature, add the rennet. It's very important to keep an eye on the temperature because if the milk is too hot the curd for the cheese will be too coarse. If the temperature is too low the curd will be too fragile to form. It's a delicate art!

Turn off the heat and leave the mixture to set for 1 hour. At this stage, the curd will cut like junket, and you should be able to stand a whisk upright in it.

My *commare* makes the sign of the cross over the cauldron before breaking up the curd with a large whisk. I wonder whether this step is essential, but hey, her recipe always works! Whisk the curd gently to form a fine mush – this will take approximately 5 minutes. Make sure you whisk enough, because otherwise the cheese will be coarse.

Now you need to separate the curd (*tuma*) from the whey (*acciata*). This is done by pressing down gently on the mixture with two of the cheese baskets (*fascile*) and then gently coaxing the curd to one side of the cauldron with your open hand and outstretched fingers. Once you have all the curd against one side, you then push it all to the opposite side, making sure not to leave any crumbs of curd in the whey. If you have any difficulty settling the curd, you can precipitate it faster by adding 2–3 litres of hot water and waiting a few minutes.

Collect the curd and place in it mounds in the three cheese baskets. Press the curd in with your hands, adding more if necessary. To encourage it to bind, be like a good parent: firm but gentle! Rotate the cheese basket and press the mounded curd towards the centre and then press down from above. Try not to crumble the curd or break it up, as it will not rebind. If you want to, you can add whole black peppercorns as you add the curd to the baskets. Once the forms of

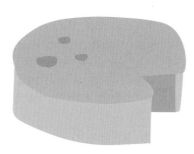

cheese seem firm and you have distributed the curd evenly, tip them out of the baskets back into the whey to seal, then turn the cheeses upside down and back into the baskets without breaking them.

At this stage, stack the cheeses on top of each other on a tray in their baskets. This will exert weight on them and express some of the excess whey. After 5 minutes, tip the forms out and turn them upside down in the baskets, then put the one that was on the bottom at the top, and vice versa. Repeat this a further six or seven times.

Use a strainer to collect any stray pieces of curd left in the whey in the cauldron (add these to your cheese forms), then place the cauldron back on the heat. Once the temperature of the whey reaches approximately 60–70°C, drop the forms of cheese in their baskets, one at a time, into the whey and leave for 1–2 minutes. This will firm them up and help them maintain their shape. Allow the forms to drain.

Now bring the whey back to the boil to make the ricotta (see page 170).

Leave the cheeses to drain for 12 hours, then remove each one from its basket and thoroughly (but gently, so you don't break the cheese) rub a dessertspoon of salt onto each side. Return the cheeses to their baskets and place any salt that has fallen off back onto the centre of each cheese. Place the baskets over a container to collect the liquid that will drain off, which you will use to cure the cheese later.

Leave the cheeses like this for 3 days, checking to see if there is any salt left on top (if there isn't, turn the cheeses over in their baskets) and basting with the salty liquid that has collected in the container. After 3 days, remove the cheeses from their baskets, rub each cheese with a pinch of salt and the salty whey, then place on a wooden plank in a cool place. Now the curing process begins, which can be a bit tedious, but it's worth it.

For the next 7 days, dip your hand in the salty whey that has drained from the cheeses and rub the cheeses all over, adding a pinch of salt to both sides as you turn and rub with the salty liquid. After a week has passed, just use the liquid to rub the cheeses each day.

After a few weeks, the cheeses will take on a slightly golden colour. At this stage, you progress to rubbing a little milk (approximately 2 teaspoons) with a pinch of salt into the cheeses daily for 1 week. Make sure your cheeses are a nice golden colour before you start doing this – if you use the milk too early, or you have not put on enough salt, the cheeses will absorb the milk and can actually expand and crack. If this happens, just use some soft commercial cheese to fill in the gaps and add a little more salt to the flat surfaces of the cheese. This will draw out some fluid and deflate the form.

After a week of curing with milk, go back to rubbing with the salty liquid and continue doing this for a further 1–2 months. After that, begin to rub every 3–4 days with a mixture of olive oil and milk. The oil is used to stop the surface from going mouldy and also to slow down the drying out of the cheese. The cheese can now be eaten, but as it actually ferments during the curing process, if eaten too early it will have a rancid yeasty flavour rather than the rich, mature flavour you want. (See notes on keeping cheeses long-term, page 178.)

At about 6 months, the cheese will be quite sharp and ready to be used straight away for grating, or to be sealed in paraffin wax or in vacuum-sealed bags to keep for eating later. Before putting on the wax, make sure you scrape off any mould if it has formed on the surface of the cheese.

Variations

Pepper cheese
Formaggio pepato

Add peppercorns to your cheese when first placing it into the baskets (as described opposite). However, first pour boiling water over the peppercorns and leave them to stand for 2–3 minutes. This will sterilise them and prevent any fungal infections or spoiling of the curd.

Chilli cheese
Formaggio piccanti

Add dried chilli flakes to the fresh curd when putting it into the baskets or rub in finely ground chilli powder with the salt when salting the forms for the first time. The chilli will penetrate with the salt over time.

Ricotta (continued from previous page)

Bring the whey back to the boil. As it heats, a thick, coarse froth will form on top. Remove this with a slotted spoon. As the whey heats to about 80°C, a very fine, creamy froth will appear on top of the whey. At this point, pour in the 4 litres of fresh milk that you put aside and add the 500 g of salt. Now slowly bring the lot to the boil, constantly but gently moving the whey around with a long stick (such as a clean broom handle). Rather than stirring the whey, just tap the stick on the bottom of the cauldron. Just before the ricotta begins to form, a firm, foamy layer will begin to appear on the surface. As the whey comes to boiling point, the ricotta will form from the bottom surface of the cauldron. The tapping will free the ricotta from the base and allow it to float to the surface. The sound that the tapping makes will change from a high tone to a lower tone, much like a broken clay pot. Stop tapping at this point. The layer of firm ricotta floating on the surface will fold inwards from the edge of the cauldron. Reduce the heat to low.

Have 2–3 litres of cold water handy; every time the milk starts to boil through the layer of ricotta, pour in a little of the cold water. This sudden coldness will hold the temperature just on boiling point, allowing the ricotta to continue to form.

After about 10 minutes of this, turn off the heat and allow the cauldron to stand for 15 minutes. Carefully remove the froth on top of the ricotta (this delicate froth was given to children to eat, back in the day!). At this point, my *commare* would make the sign of the cross three times over the cauldron too. Now, with a slotted spoon, gently collect the ricotta, which will have formed in a 7–10 cm thick layer on top. What is left is the whey, which you can also eat by soaking fresh bread in the liquid.

Traditionally, the ricotta would then be placed into moulds handmade from reeds by the local basketmaker – however, nowadays we use plastic moulds! Eat the ricotta while it is still warm. It is totally different to the week-old ricotta you buy in the shops.

Variations

Salted ricotta
Ricotta salata

As you remove the freshly made ricotta from the cauldron, add approximately 1 teaspoon of salt per small container of ricotta (250 g), mixing well. You can also layer some finely ground Dried Hot Chillies (see page 109) or chilli powder at this stage, so when you eventually cut the cured ricotta, it will have an interesting grain of red chilli through the centre. Place the ricotta into perforated plastic containers, such as clean butter or margarine containers with about 20 holes made in the bottom and sides. Leave to drain for 2–3 days.

Rub the surface gently with a little of the brine that has formed and place in a warm, draughty spot to allow the ricotta to dry (this is important as the ricotta may become mouldy if it doesn't dry quickly enough). Make sure to keep it protected from birds if you place it outside – they love it!

The salted ricotta can be eaten after 2–3 weeks, at which time it is a very buttery, soft cheese. Alternatively, it can be left to dry for approximately 8–10 weeks, at which point it can be grated onto pasta. To prevent the ricotta from drying out any further, place it in small clean jars (see steps 1–2, page 21) and cover with oil, ensuring the ricotta is completely submerged. You can also add a chilli, dried bay leaf or some dried capsicum to add to the flavour and appearance.

Ricotta made from fresh pasteurised milk

Ricotta con latte fresco pasteurizzato

You do not need to have access to a cow to make fresh ricotta. And there are many different ways of curdling the milk, such as using lemon juice, vinegar, fig sap (see page 167), junket tablets or even whey that has gone off.

Basic recipe

4 litres non-homogenised full-cream
    organic milk
1 tablespoon table salt
juice of 1 lemon, 4 cm fig stem
    or 1 junket tablet

Variations

With lemon
Con limone

Slowly heat the milk, stirring constantly, until it is almost at boiling point and a fine froth has formed on top. Add the salt. To test if the temperature is right to add the lemon juice, remove some milk with a spoon and add a drop of lemon juice to it. If it's ready, the milk will curdle immediately. At this point, add the remaining lemon juice. Stir with the handle of a wooden spoon. At this point, the milk will begin to curdle. Turn the heat down to its lowest setting and leave for 4–5 minutes. If the milk begins to boil through the curds forming on top, add a little cold water. After 5 minutes, the ricotta will have formed on the surface. Remove the curds with a slotted spoon and place into perforated containers to drain. This ricotta will have a slight taste of lemon, which is not at all unpleasant. Eat while still warm.

With a fig branch
Con ramo di fico

Be very careful when handling fig sap, as it can irritate or burn the skin. This method only works when figs are in season and the sap is flowing, usually between October and March.

Heat the milk to just below boiling point, as opposite, and add the salt.

Slice the stem of the fig and dilute the sap in a small amount of water. To test the temperature of the milk, remove some milk on a spoon and add the fig stem. It should curdle immediately. At this point, add the sap and the stem to the milk and stir gently. After 2–3 minutes, the milk will begin to curdle. Turn off the heat and leave for 5 minutes. Remove the fig stem. Gently ladle the ricotta into perforated containers and allow to drain. Eat while still warm.

With junket tablets

This is the simplest method, which really produces a cottage cheese (that tastes like ricotta!). Bring the milk almost to the boil, until it has a nice cooked aroma. Add the salt and allow the milk to cool to about 39°C (until the milk is warm to touch). In a separate glass, dissolve the junket tablet in water. Add the dissolved tablet to the warm milk and leave to set until you can stand a spoon upright in it. At this point, break up the curd with the handle of a wooden spoon. Once the curd is broken up, allow it to sit for a few minutes, then ladle into perforated containers. Eat while still warm.

Mozzarella and provolone

The secret to making mozzarella is the bacteria in the milk, which is needed to produce an acid environment so that the milk will form curds. These bacteria are added to the milk at the beginning, either as an acid or whey. This is collected after the cheese is made. The whey is not turned into ricotta but instead allowed to stand on the kitchen bench overnight. The whey will be slightly 'off' but will have produced the bacteria that is needed.

Alternatively, you can simply add yoghurt and buttermilk to the milk. These products contain a range of acid-producing bacteria that can be used to make mozzarella. I prefer this process as it is more predictable!

4 litres fresh unpasteurised milk (ideally water buffalo milk, but cow or goat will do)
3 tablespoons fresh natural yoghurt (containing live cultures such as lactobacillus acidophilus, lactobacillus bulgaris and/or streptococcus thermophilus)
3 tablespoons fresh buttermilk
1 teaspoon rennet
table salt

Special equipment
large stainless-steel stockpot or cauldron
thermometer
pH meter or litmus paper

Pour the milk into the large stainless-steel stockpot or cauldron over medium heat and warm to 32°C. Add the yoghurt, buttermilk and rennet. Turn off the heat and allow to stand for 45 minutes to curdle. Cut the curd into squares, like a chessboard, making sure your knife reaches all the way down to the bottom of the pot or cauldron. Stir for 5 minutes, trying not to break up the squares of curd too much, then remove from the heat and allow to stand for 15 minutes. Pour off the whey and reserve it either to make ricotta (see page 170) or for your next batch of mozzarella. You can freeze whey for 6–12 months.

Cover with a cloth and leave the curd to sit at room temperature to allow time for the bacteria to produce the right acidity. Unless the pH of the curd is 5.3, it will not stretch. You can monitor the pH with a pH meter or litmus paper. This process can take anywhere from a few hours to overnight. Do not be tempted to go to the next step until the pH is correct, as it will not work. To check if it is ready, heat 200 ml of water to 85°C, drop in a lump of curd and stir. Test by pulling and folding the curd. If it softens, draws into strings and is glossy, it is ready. If it breaks, it is not.

Once the curd is ready, cut it into 2 cm blocks and place in a shallow saucepan. Heat 2 litres of water to 85°C. Pour this over the curd and stir with a wooden spoon. The temperature of the water should stay between 57°C and 60°C. As the curd warms, it will become stringy.

Put on a pair of thick rubber gloves to avoid burning your hands. Press and cut the hot curd into balls the size of large lemons. Stretch and fold each ball over itself, over and over again. The balls should be glossy and smooth on the outside, and layered on the inside. Plunge the balls into a cold diluted brine of 1 tablespoon of salt per 1 litre of water. They can be kept in the fridge for up to 1 week and eaten fresh.

My favourite way to eat fresh mozzarella? 'Caprese' style, with sliced garden-fresh tomatoes, basil leaves and a pungent olive oil, sprinkled with salt and pepper. This is absolute heaven!

Alternatively, the mozzarella can be placed in a concentrated salt brine (230 g of salt per 1 litre of water) and kept in the fridge for 1–3 days, after which time the cheese can be

smoked for 3–4 hours with hickory chips (see smoking instructions, page 201). Hang to cure for 2–3 weeks and rub the surface daily with olive oil to prevent cracking. These firmer *mozzarelle* are suitable to eat with bread or to use on pizzas.

To make provolone or *caciocavallo* (so called because the two forms of cheese were draped over the horse's back like a saddle), simply add 1 tablespoon of lipase (an enzyme present in raw milk, which you can buy in powdered form from specialist suppliers) for every 4 litres of milk at the beginning. Cut the curd into much larger balls (about the size of a grapefruit or larger). Plunge into the cold diluted brine until firm, then place in a concentrated brine (230 g of salt per 1 litre of water) for 3 days at 10°C. Hang to cure in a cool place (ideally 10°C with 85 per cent humidity) for about 3 weeks. Remember to continue to rub the surface daily with olive oil to prevent cracking and mould formation. After 3 weeks, clean the surface with diluted salty water, pat dry and cover with wax (see page 178). Store in a cool place and allow to ripen for 3–12 months. The longer the curing, the sharper the flavour.

Happy provoloning!

Pecorino

This is a fairly straightforward cheese to make at home using non-homogenised, full-cream organic milk you can buy at the supermarket. And you can also make ricotta at the same time!

If you are making a harder, sharper cheese for grating, allow the milk to stand in the fridge overnight and remove the cream, putting it aside to add to the whey when making ricotta later on. If you want to make a moister cheese that is better eaten fresh, then use the whole milk with the cream.

20 litres non-homogenised full-cream organic milk
250 g natural yoghurt (containing live cultures such as lactobacillus acidophilus, lactobacillus bulgaris and/or streptococcus thermophilus)
1 teaspoon lipase powder, dissolved in 250 ml water (optional, see method)
1 teaspoon rennet
170 g table salt

Special equipment
large stainless-steel stockpot or cauldron
thermometer
pH meter or litmus paper
3 × 1 kg plastic cheese baskets
plastic cheese coating (available from specialist cheese shops)

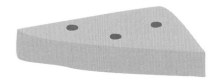

Pour the milk into the large stainless-steel stockpot or cauldron and heat to 37°C. Add the yoghurt or starter.

If you are using the skimmed milk to end up with a harder, sharper cheese, add the lipase now. If you are using the full-cream milk and want a softer, fresher cheese, you do not need to add lipase.

Next, remove 100 ml of milk from the pot or cauldron, mix with the rennet, then return to the pot or cauldron. Mix for 2–3 minutes. Heat the mixture for 30–35 minutes, making sure the temperature is kept at 37°C. At this stage, the curd will have set so that you can stand a spoon upright in it.

As you would for mozzarella, cut the curd into squares, like a chessboard, making sure your knife reaches all the way down to the bottom of the pot or cauldron. Leave to settle for 5–8 minutes. This will allow the curd to begin shrinking and expel the whey. Now stir the mixture again to break up any lumps. At this stage, measure the pH of the mixture, which should be between 6.45 and 6.5.

Gradually heat up the curd again until it reaches 45°C. You should do this really slowly so that it takes about 50 minutes to get the mixture from around 31°C to 45°C. Once it reaches that temperature, stir briskly.

Wearing thick rubber gloves, take a handful of the curd and squeeze firmly. Shake your fist a few times by your side to flick off any excess whey from the curd. Squeeze your hand again. The curd should be firm and not squeeze out through the fingers of your closed fist. If it does, stir the curd again and allow it to sit for a further 5 minutes, then repeat this test.

Once the curd is firm, allow it to settle in the cauldron for 3–4 minutes. Remove the curd with a fine metal strainer, place it in a large bowl or container, and save the whey to make ricotta (see page 170).

Now you need to salt the curd.

Dissolve the salt in a saucepan with 400 ml of water, then bring to the boil. Allow the mixture to cool, then splash onto the curd and mix it in with your hands. Remove the curd using a fine metal strainer (you will have about 2 kg from this quantity of milk) and divide it evenly between two of the cheese baskets. Sit one basket on top of the other and place the third (empty) basket on top of them – sit a 1 litre container of water inside the empty basket to weigh the baskets down. After 5 minutes, rotate the bottom basket to the top; repeat this process three times. After 20 minutes, flip the curd over within the baskets and rotate the order of the baskets again. Repeat this process hourly over 4 hours.

Remove the cheeses from the baskets and place on a wire rack overnight in a warm (roughly 20°C) place.

After 24 hours, remove the cheeses from the wire rack and place on a fine plastic rack (for instance, a length of clean gutter guard) that will allow air circulation around the cheeses and prevent mould formation. Turn the cheeses over every day for 3 days. By this stage, the cheeses should have developed a slightly golden colour. Brush the surfaces with a coat of plastic cheese coating (which you can obtain from specialist suppliers).

Once they are coated, store the cheeses in a cool, dry place (roughly 14°C with 75–80 per cent humidity). Turn the cheeses over every 2 days for the first 8 days and then every week for a further 2 months. Cheese making is not for the impatient, that's for sure!

After 2 months, the cheese will be quite soft and mild, and ready to be eaten. If you want a sharper, drier cheese for grating over pasta and the like (similar to parmesan) it will need to dry for approximately 8 months. Make it at Easter and it will be ready for Christmas!

Variations and extras

With pepper
Con pepato

Use 20–40 whole black peppercorns, depending on how strong you like it. Boil the peppercorns in 400 ml of water for a few minutes, then drain and allow to cool. Add to the curd and mix before you add the brine for salting. Note that if you do this, you cannot use the whey to make ricotta as it will have a peppery flavour!

Making ricotta from the whey

Measure how much whey you have – from the original 20 litres of milk, you should have about 10 litres of whey – and then pour it into a large stockpot that is twice as high as it is wide. This will increase the yield! Heat the whey to 62°C, stirring regularly. Remove any froth and particles that come to the surface with a fine metal strainer.

Add 20 per cent of your whey's volume of full-cream milk (or the cream that you have put aside from the earlier cheese making). So, if you have 10 litres of whey, you will add 2 litres of milk or cream. Add sea salt to taste and heat to 95°C, stirring constantly. Do not let it boil.

For every 10 litres of whey, dilute about 20 ml of white wine vinegar or cider vinegar in 100 ml of water. Add to the whey, stir quickly and when fine particles begin to float to the surface, stop stirring. Allow to simmer for at least 5 minutes at 95°C.

Place your ricotta containers in a sink or basin with some cold water at the bottom. Gently scoop out the solid floating curds from the simmering whey with a fine metal strainer and place into the containers. The cold water will stop the ricotta from draining out.

Allow to drain for 1 hour, then eat straight away, warm, with fresh bread. Fantastic!

Keeping cheeses long-term

Once your cheeses are hard and dry enough, you need to stop them continuing to dry out; otherwise they'll just become hard and inedible (although you may still be able to grate them). Don't let your labour of love go to waste!

There are several different methods for keeping cheeses long-term:

Placing them under oil
This is done mainly with fresh and soft cheeses. The oil can be flavoured with fresh or dried herbs, if you like.

Covering the form with wax
This is done mainly with harder cheeses used for grating. Cheese wax can be purchased from specialist suppliers.

Placing them in a vacuum-sealed bag
These are great little devices that maintain the cheese at the right moisture level, and also allow the cheese to continue to mature.

CURED MEATS

SALUMI

10

'Cu si marita e cuntentu nu iornu, cu mmazza nu porcu e cuntentu n'annu.'
(Those who marry are happy for one day, but kill a pig and you're happy all year.)
– Calabrese proverb

There must be as many recipes for salamis as there are Italians. This is a reflection of our competitive nature and how we all think our family's version is 'the best', even if the recipe only differs by a mere gram of fennel seed! Family recipes are often secret or only shared with a select few.

I remember well when I was living on a farm in Swan Hill as a young child. My father had a number of *compari*, all of whom, like us, raised pigs for meat. Every year, after the main work season was over, there would begin a round robin of the annual killing of the pigs; each weekend, one of the group would slaughter his pig and everyone else would help out.

The day would begin with the women putting on a large cauldron of boiling water and the men fetching the pig. A squeal would be heard up and down the road as the pig was slaughtered. The women would collect the blood and take it away; the men would begin butchering the carcass. Every part of the pig was saved and put aside for use. Even the entrails were collected and cleaned, to be used as the casings for the salamis. There was a frenzy of activity as the meat was cut up, with everyone giving advice on the best way to do this or that. A second cauldron was set up for all the bits and bones to be thrown in and boiled down – this would be eaten that evening with some wine and olives (see *Frittuli,* page 191).

By the end of the day, Dad would have given most of his pig away to his friends. He knew, however, that over the following weeks he would receive as much back as he had given away. Also, he would be able to taste each person's efforts at outperforming everyone else in the group as far as cured meats went!

This system obviously required a certain amount of trust, or else one would end up short. I have another *compare* who was short-changed a number of years in a row and decided thereafter that he would make two sets of salamis – the first for house consumption, the second for sharing with his *compari*. The second was made up of half meat and half hot chilli. When his friends came around, he would bring out the 'special' second salamis and generously offer to give them away, but warning that they were a 'little hot' that year. Invariably his guests would decline the offer, explaining that they had stomach problems, or that the doctor had told them to watch their *colesterolo*, and so he would keep his full complement of salamis!

In Italy, the traditional time to make salamis is the day after Christmas. When I visited the family of my *compare* Rennie in Pordenone, we arrived on the day of the kill. The pigs had been killed in the stables and Nives (the aunty) was carrying in cold water from the well. The men began butchering the meat and adding the spices. Bizarrely, a little dried animal urine was scraped off the walls of the stables and also added to the meat. It was explained that this contains nitrate, which helps preserve the meat and keep it red! Nothing is wasted, not even the urine.

It was intensely cold and damp in the stables and we consumed two bottles of grappa for every pig slaughtered. Needless to say, I had a grandfather of a hangover the next day!

Making your own salami at home

So how does one go about making salami *in casa* (at home)? Firstly, you need to make sure that the pig you buy (or raise) has been properly fed on vegetables, fruit and, for the last two months of its life, a mixture of barley, oats and acorns. This will ensure that the meat is dry and deep red in colour. Dairy-fed or battery pigs have a pink meat that is very moist and lean; it is not suitable for salamis, as it dries too quickly and is very bland to eat. If you cannot raise your own pigs, and I understand that a number of inner-city councils have an objection to this, there are many butchers who have specialised for the salami market, so shop around.

The ideal weight for a pig is around 120 kg. This ensures that the pig is lean but with enough fat to make a good salami blend. There should be at least a 1.5 cm layer of fat along the back and the leg. If you get a larger pig, there will be too much fat waste. Sows that have had a litter, for example, are not suitable for good salamis.

Normally, a butcher slaughters the pig. Request that the blood be put aside for you. This needs to be whisked while still draining and warm to ensure that it does not clot, then refrigerated for use later on. You will also need the head, liver, lungs, heart and the 'veil', which is the lining of the abdominal cavity that you will use to wrap pancetta and *capocollo*.

You will also need plenty of salt, black peppercorns and various spices; a collection of sharp knives; a large, clean work surface; at least one 10 litre plastic container and a large rubbish bin. Finally, you need a large stockpot or cauldron to make the *Coppa di Testa* (see page 215) and *Frittuli* (see page 191).

When planning to make the salamis the traditional way, always make sure that the moon is on the increase (in other words, it is coming up to a new or full moon) and that rain or moist conditions have been forecast for the next few days. Do not make the salamis if the weather forecast is for dry, mild conditions (see the section on hanging salamis, page 191). It's also a good idea to ensure that any friends who will be helping you are experienced with butchery, or are at least aware of how to handle very sharp knives. You don't want anyone cutting off a finger! (This is not necessarily bad for the salamis, but your friends tend not to come back the following year to help.)

The pig has to be slaughtered, cleaned, split in half and hung overnight. Choose a cold and frosty night as the cold will harden the fat, making its removal much easier. Make sure you warn the family members that the garage has been temporarily converted into a chilling room, or you may end up with some distressed younger people should they stumble across it after a night of partying!

The next morning is an early start. It is essential that your helpers arrive at 5 am. There is a long day ahead and you need to sell it to your friends and family as a transcultural experience, which is essential for them to understand your heritage. What I tend to do is to describe this as a day of excitement and festivities to my unsuspecting friends, and ask them to turn up with knives ready and not a clue as to what is involved. The fact that they get an insight into my culture and heritage is a bonus! I make sure to only invite a few friends at a time, or else no one will be around to help me the following year.

Butchering the pig

Firstly, you need to remove the head and the prosciutto (the back quarter of the pig) as this is cured with the skin. Next, remove the pancetta (in Calabria and Puglia, the pancetta is removed with the skin). This is removed from the middle of the chest, lifting the meat off the ribs so that you end up with a slab of meat, some layers of fat and skin.

If you want to make *Zampone* (stuffed lower leg of pork), you will also need to remove the skin off the front legs, down to and including the toenail, all in one piece. Next, remove the shoulder, being careful not to cut into the *capocollo*, which is along the spine at the neck.

At this stage, what you will have left is a number of pieces of meat with skin on. Remove the skin from all of the meat except for the prosciutto and the pancetta. Be careful not to remove any fat at this stage. If you cut some fat off with the skin, separate it and put the skin and fat aside. The fat from the back of the pig along the spine is a soft, sweet fat that needs to be removed separately as it will be used for the salamis and *soppresse*. Clean the skin and set aside.

As mentioned above, the fat along the back has a fine texture and ensures that the salamis do not have any stringy strands that get caught between your teeth. Remove and set aside the fat from the back to approximately two-thirds of the way down the side of the pig towards the lower abdomen. Collect and discard the fat along the underbelly, as this is not good enough quality to consume. Or you can keep this fat to make soap (see page 221).

Next, remove the *capocollo*. This is the dark red meat at the neck next to the spine, from the base of the head down to the beginning of the fifth rib. Cut the meat along the spine and off the bone. You will know when to stop, because the meat will change from a deep red to a lighter pink. Only use the darker meat. Place the two pieces of meat in a 10 litre plastic container and cover with a cloth (to stop flies from getting to it) until you are ready to salt the meat.

Now remove the remaining meat from the shoulder, the ribs and the rest of the carcass. If you want to make *soppresse*, the best meat for this is off the leg, so you will end up with one or two less *prosciutti*. The rest of the meat is ideal for sausages and salamis (note: if you are only using a half pig, don't be too concerned about separating all the meats).

If you have not already done so, remove the skin from the pancetta (unless you are going to make Calabrese-style pancetta, see page 201). Remove any extra fat and place the flaps of meat in with the *capocolli*.

Next, prepare the prosciutto (see page 202) and put aside any trimmed meat and fat to be made into salamis. As you remove the rest of the meat from the bone, make sure that you also remove any excess fat and place it to one side.

If there is any meat that has tendons or fibrous material or blood around it, remove this and place it to one side. This pile of meat is not good for salamis, as it will make them stringy and unpleasant to eat, but it is fine to use for fresh sausages.

So now you should have:

* Two piles of meat – one that is clean, lean and free of sinews and tendons (for salamis and *soppresse*), and a second that is sinewy and bloody (for fresh sausages, liver sausages, *cotechino* and so on)
* Two piles of fat – one from the upper two-thirds (closer to the spine) of the pig (for salamis and *soppresse*), and a second from the lower part (towards the teats) for fresh sausages, liver sausages and *cotechino*
* Two *capocolli*, two *pancette* and two *prosciutti* (unless you are going to use one or both of these for *soppresse*)
* The skin of the pig (from this you will need to remove and reserve all excess fat; this is good fat for salamis)
* The head, trotters, heart, liver, lungs and kidneys.

If you are brave, you will also have the whisked blood, and any leftover fat can be used to make soap (see page 221).

Every region in Italy, and every family within that region, has its own recipes for salamis. I have had a fantastic time collecting some of these recipes and grouping them together. As long as the right amount of salt is used and the curing process is maintained, you can vary the recipes almost at will.

You need 28–30 g of salt for every 1 kg of meat when making salamis and sausages, to ensure they don't spoil. It is essential that you only use sea salt for the salamis; never use iodised salt as this will interfere with the curing process.

As for other preservatives, such as sodium nitrate (Chile saltpetre), this is a very debatable topic. Sodium nitrate is often added to salamis to maintain their deep pink colour and to preserve the meat once it is cut. However, it is carcinogenic, so an alternative is to use mined rock salt. The latter has a certain amount of impurities, but contains only a small amount of sodium nitrate.

I am going to start with the recipe for Calabrese salami here, to illustrate the process, and because it's the one I make most often! But you can use any other salami recipe in this book at this stage in the process.

Calabrese salami

Salame del Calabria

Calabrese salami is distinctive because of the additions of Hot Chilli Paste (see page 122) or powder, Capsicum Paste (see page 122) and fresh fennel seeds. These give the salamis their characteristic colour and flavour.

Did you know that chillies have preservative qualities? A fact that any Calabrese will demonstrate due to their great skin and youthful looks from a life of eating hot chillies!

lean pork meat and soft fat from the back of the pig (see pages 187–188; 80% meat and 20% fat)
sea salt
freshly ground black pepper
fennel seeds
chilli powder
Capsicum Paste (see page 122)
red wine or grappa (optional)
pre-soaked lamb's bungs (see page 190)

Special equipment
meat mincer
string
large safety pin
size 14 elastic netting
meat hooks

Remove and separate the meat as described on pages 187–188.

Pass the lean meat through the meat mincer on the coarse setting (the grid with four holes). As you mince the meat, mix in some fat from along the spine (which is very soft and has no fibre/sinew). The final salami mixture needs to be four parts lean meat to one part fat. A variation is to add fat in small cubes at the mixing stage (see below) rather than mince it with the meat. This (ironically) makes the salamis leaner and firmer to cut.

The amount of added fat will vary depending on the leanness of the pig. If the pig is particularly lean, you may have to get extra fat from the butcher. If the pig is fatty (as seen by the thickness of the layer of fat along the back, which is ideally 1.5–2 cm thick), then you won't need to add as much fat, as there will be plenty in the meat off the chest and abdomen.

Mix the minced lean meat and fat well, then spread out flat on a large, plastic-covered table.

For every 1 kg of mince, add 28–30 g of sea salt, 3 g of freshly ground black pepper, 1 g of fennel seeds and up to 1 g of chilli powder (this will vary according to your taste). Next, add 30 ml of capsicum paste and 20 ml of red wine or grappa (if using) per 1 kg of meat.

The capsicum paste is prepared in late summer (see page 122). If you don't want to make the capsicum paste, you can substitute sweet paprika instead at a rate of 10 g per 1 kg of meat, or buy a commercially made capsicum paste. The capsicum paste (or paprika, if that's what you end up using) produces beautiful red oil when you cut the mature salami.

Mix well with your hands, kneading the mince with the heel of your palm at least three or four times, from one side of the table to the other. When you're finished, the mince should feel sticky and very well combined. Leave for a minimum of 4 hours to allow the spices to flavour the mince.

To test for flavour, take a small amount of the mince and fry in a dry frying pan. When cooked, taste it. It should be relatively salty and have a pronounced flavour of fennel and chilli. If not, add more of each and mix again. This is the first reward for your unsuspecting helpers, so make a big ceremony of it. Throw in a glass of good wine and you may have a chance of redeeming yourself, as you all sit round with the freshly cooked salami mince and some crusty bread.

Leave the mince on the table overnight, covered well with a cloth. At this stage, all your friends, and particularly your children, will have remembered some essential previous engagement and make their excuses. It's understandable – the next job is a smelly one and I would not test even the closest friendship with it! So, farewell your friends and prepare the bungs ready for the next day (see overleaf).

Bungs

Bungs are made from the intestines of animals. Originally, the pigs' own intestines would be used to encase the salamis but now, mercifully, they can be bought from a butcher. They need to be ordered well ahead and the better ones are freshly salted. The older ones tend to turn slightly black and do not become white and clear with washing.

You will need some thin sausage skins, some *cacciatore* skins (these are slightly bigger than sausage skins and make smaller salamis that dry faster), approximately 20 lamb's bungs and, if you want to make *soppresse*, three or four ox bungs. Remember that the bigger the salami, the fewer total salamis you end up with. I tend to make approximately 10 to 15 lamb's bung salamis, four to six lengths of sausages, about 20 *cacciatore* (they dry quickly for early use) and one or two *soppresse*. This will obviously vary on the size of the pig and the number of *capocollo*, pancetta and *prosciutti* that you decide to make too. Chat to your butcher about the best size and quantity of bungs to use if unsure.

Firstly, separate the bungs and place them in a bucket with warm water and four or five sliced lemons. This will remove some of the smell and slightly bleach the skins. Fill the bungs with warm water and allow to soak. After a couple of hours, rinse another three or four times in warm water. Turn the bungs inside out and allow them to soak overnight in a fresh bucket of warm water with lemon slices.

The next day, you are ready to make your salamis and hopefully your friends will turn up again (or you have invited a new group of friends, who have no idea what you got up to the day before!). The meat should be ready. The sign of well-seasoned meat is that it sticks together like well-kneaded dough when pressed into a ball.

The meat can be pressed into the bungs with a hand-operated sausage mincer, without the mincing blade or the plate, or by using a specially designed sausage filler called an '*insaccatrice*', which makes life very easy. While you can use implements to help, this process really needs to be done by hand as you have much better control over the rate of filling of the bungs, and the meat will not be bruised.

When filling the bungs, make sure that they are very firmly packed. If they are loose, they will have air pockets and will tend to become mouldy inside. If you use the '*insaccatrice*', this tends not to be a problem. You will most likely burst a few of the bungs as you assess the pressure needed. Don't worry, it's all part of the learning experience! If you are making *cacciatore*, fill to approximately 30 centimetres in length. Lamb's bungs should be filled to just below the small hole at the top end of the bung.

Tie all of your bungs firmly (double tie with strong string to prevent the sausages and salamis from slipping and falling onto the ground once hung). Once all the sausages and salamis are filled, pierce the skins with a large safety pin 10 to 20 times (or you can get dedicated salami piercers from specialist suppliers). Allow the sausages and salamis to sit for approximately two to three hours before hanging. I tie my sausages every 10 centimetres.

If you have any leftover bungs, you can re-salt them or freeze them, but I don't do this anymore after we ended up with what my wife thought was chicken meat in our soup ... but no, they were bungs (it was not a very happy night).

When ready to hang, place the salamis (not the sausages or *cacciatore*, as they dry quicker) in elastic netting, which is available from the butcher in different sizes for different uses. Size 12 is used to enclose the small salamis, size 14 for the lamb's bungs and size 16 for the *capocollo*, pancetta and *soppresse*. Netting ensures that the salamis remain firm with continuing pressure as they dry. If you don't use netting, after the first week of drying place all the *soppresse* and salamis (not the *cacciatore* and sausages) on a bench and place a heavy weight on top for two weeks to ensure that there are no air pockets in the centre.

Next you make your *cotechine*, fresh sausages and liver sausages.

Finally, make the *Frittuli*. Cut up the bones and cut the pig's skin into strips that are approximately two centimetres thick and five centimetres long. Place the bones and skin in a large stockpot or cauldron with the trotters (reserve one if you want to make *Zampone*, see page 198) and any small leftover pieces of stringy meat. Add salt, freshly ground black pepper, a couple of roughly chopped onions and one litre of water, then slowly bring to the boil. Reduce to a simmer, then cook for two hours, during which time you will hang the sausages and salamis and clean up. At the end of the night, you eat the *Frittuli* hot, with Hot Chillies in Vinegar (see page 58) and fresh bread. Plenty of wine is needed to cut through the salty, gelatinous, sticky bits of meat attached to juicy bones. Make sure that you allow the juices to dribble down your forearm to your elbow. This is heaven.

Hanging and curing the salamis

Make sure that the place where you hang the salamis is cool, with moisture in the air (approximately 60–80 per cent) and only a very slight draught, ideally no air movement at all. Hang the salamis on meat hooks so that the skins do not touch – this will allow them to dry evenly. It is absolutely essential that the salamis do not dry too quickly. You must hang the salamis away from iron roofing, preferably just off the ground where the air is cool and stable. A *compare* from Delianova, who is a florist, stores his salamis in the cool room with the flowers!

During the first week, the salamis may develop a slight mouldy covering. Don't worry, it won't harm you; just wipe it off with a mixture of olive oil and vinegar every couple of days. If you want to give the sausages an extra flavour, at about day four you can smoke them for two days using hickory chips (see smoking instructions, page 201).

The first four weeks of curing are absolutely critical. It is during this initial period that the salamis begin their natural fermentation or curing process. As always, when we transport a custom to another country and the conditions change, it isn't always possible to get the same results following traditional methods.

For example, Australian winters can be very dry, with overnight frosts and zero per cent humidity – very different from the normal moist and foggy winter conditions in Italy where our traditions began.

The most common failure with salamis is that they dry too quickly and therefore develop a hard outer rim of dried meat, becoming empty inside as they dry.

Some tips for salami drying

* Make sure that you hang the salamis away from the roof (so heat cannot be conducted); preferably hang them close to the ground.
* Make sure that the humidity is between 60 to 80 per cent. This can be maintained by placing moist sawdust on the ground.
* Ensure that there is minimal or ideally no draught.
* Do not be concerned about any mould. It is a good sign as it means that the humidity is adequate.

After four to six weeks (depending on the humidity of the room), the thin sausages will be ready to eat. They will be firm and, on cutting, a deep red. The *cacciatore* will take eight to 10 weeks and the salamis approximately 12 weeks. The *soppresse* can take up to one year, becoming better and tastier as time passes.

Once the salamis are firm and cured, they can be kept from continuing to harden and dry by using one of the following methods:

* Placing them in large jars and covering completely with extra-virgin olive oil. If using this method it is essential that the salami mix is a little leaner. Do not prick the skins before hanging if you are going to use this preservation method as this tends to make the salamis oily after a while.
* Wiping them with a generous amount of extra-virgin olive oil and placing them in large jars with a few centimetres of oil at the bottom. Every so often, say weekly, agitate the jars so that the oil coats the salamis. This keeps the salamis moist without becoming too oily. Again, do not prick the skins if you want to use this method.
* Covering them with wheat. This is done in the Abruzzi and is very effective, although the salamis still tend to keep drying, albeit very slowly.
* Wrapping them in brown paper, then covering in white ash. A friend in Tuscany does this!
* Sealing them by dipping in melted wax. This is a fairly modern method. Cheese wax can be purchased from specialist suppliers for this purpose.
* Placing them in vacuum-sealed bags. This is probably the best method as it keeps them moist but prevents any further drying.

Salamis

Venetian salami

Salame del Veneto

My friend Dino Bertolin is a fourth-generation *salumista* living in Melbourne, who has won the Springvale Italian community club salami competition eight years in a row. I had to promise that his name would be immortalised in this book to entice him to part with this secret recipe! These salamis have an intense garlic flavour that is even more enjoyable with a glass of dry white wine or grappa.

500 g garlic cloves, crushed
1.5 litres white wine
70 kg lean pork meat and soft fat from the
    back of the pig (see pages 187–188; 80%
    meat and 20% fat)
2.1 kg sea salt
210 g black pepper (a mixture of finely and
    coarsely ground)
24 pre-soaked lamb's bungs (see page 190)

Special equipment
meat mincer
string
large safety pin
size 14 elastic netting
meat hooks

The night before you mince the meat, prepare the garlic and wine mix. Soak the crushed garlic cloves in the white wine and leave to infuse overnight.

The next day, strain the garlic and wine mixture through a clean muslin bag into a bowl and set aside.

Pass the meat and fat through the mincer twice, using the plate with 1 cm holes. Spread the minced meat out flat on a large, plastic-covered table and add the salt, pepper and 1 litre of the garlic and wine mixture (save the rest for the *Cotechino*, page 211).

Mix everything together, making sure to knead the mince well. Allow the mince to rest for 2 hours. At this stage, if you roll a small ball of mince and throw it back onto the main pile, it will stick but you will still be able to remove it.

Following the instructions on pages 190–192, press the mince into the bungs, piercing the skin approximately 10 times, then place in the netting and hang. After 1 week, place a weight on the salamis to ensure that they do not have any air in the centre. Leave under the weight for 2 days, then re-hang. Leave the salamis to hang for 6–8 weeks, then try!

Variations

Abruzzese salami

Remove the meat and fat from the carcass and mince as for the Calabrese Salami (see page 189). For every 1 kg of mince, add 30 g of sea salt, 3 g of coarsely ground black pepper, 2 g of whole black peppercorns and 30 ml of white wine. Mix the mince and spices together and knead well. Leave overnight. Follow the instructions on pages 190–192 and press the mince into lamb's bungs or sausage skins, then pierce and hang. They will be ready after 4–12 weeks, depending on the thickness of the salamis.

Rivestita

Remove the pork sirloin (approximately 30 cm long). Salt as for *capocollo* (see page 199). Remove the tough white outer layer. Place the meat in a pre-soaked ox bung and fill the rest of the bung with Venetian Salami filling (see opposite) so that the sirloin is surrounded with the salami mince. Pierce the skin 10 times and hang for approximately 2 months before eating.

Cesare's Italian salami

Salame di Cesare

10 kg lean pork meat
10 kg pork belly (no skin)
2 kg pork liver
660 g sea salt
55 g freshly ground black pepper
110 g whole black peppercorns
4 g sodium nitrate (Chile saltpetre)
20 g garlic powder
55 g dried oregano
15 pre-soaked lamb's bungs (see page 190)
1 litre red wine

Special equipment
meat mincer
string
large safety pin
size 14 elastic netting
meat hooks

Mince the meats coarsely, then spread out flat on a large, plastic-covered table. Add the salt, pepper, sodium nitrate and seasonings. Mix and knead very well, then cover and stand overnight.

Following the instructions on pages 190–192, press the mince into the bungs, pierce the skins 10 to 20 times, then place in the netting and hang for up to 2 days.

Suspend the salamis over a container in which they can hang freely and not touch. Fill the container with a good-quality red wine and leave the salamis to hang in the wine for 10 days. Remove and dry. Hang as described on pages 191–192 at a temperature of 15°C with 85 per cent humidity until firm, which will take approximately 4 weeks.

Tuscan salami

Salami Toscani

On a recent trip to my friend Ciccio's, I met Armando, the local butcher. His house is the perfect Tuscan villa, with its weathered and peeling walls of soft yellow. And right next door is a concrete-mixing factory. What a tragedy! Where is the town-planning appeals tribunal when you need it?

Finely cut 10 kg of lean pork meat and 2 kg of fine fat from the back of the pig into small cubes (less than 1 cm) by hand. Spread the mixture out flat on a large, plastic-covered table. Add 300 g of sea salt, 500 g of black peppercorns (one-third left whole and two-thirds finely ground), a glass of red wine and a small handful of ground spices: nutmeg, cinnamon, allspice and cloves. Mix well, kneading the mixture like you were making bread. Following the instructions on pages 190–192, press the meat into ox bungs, pierce the skins 10 to 20 times, then place in size 16 netting and hang. After 2–3 weeks, the salamis will form a mould; don't worry about removing it. When the salamis are ready they will have shrunk from 2 kg to about 1.3–1.5 kg. This will take approximately 3 months.

Variations

Armando's salami with fennel
Finocchiona da gavriglia di Armando

To the above recipe, add a small handful of wild fennel seeds. Press the meat into ox bungs and tie three times. Prick 10 to 20 times and hang as above.

Mario's Tuscan salami
Salami Toscani da Mario

Mario uses meat from the shoulder and prosciutto, plus about 5 per cent pancetta and about 13 per cent back fat cut into 1 cm cubes. Mince the meat (not the fat) finely, then spread out flat on a large, plastic-covered table. For every 1 kg of mince, add 26 g of sea salt, 2 g of freshly ground black pepper and 3 g of whole black peppercorns. Mix well. Add the fat cubes and gently mix through, then press the mixture into ox bungs and pierce and hang as above. This produces a deep red salami with visible cubes of fat.

'In 1986, at the age of 37, I had a successful medical practice, a wonderful wife with whom I had three amazing boys, and great friends. I felt blessed indeed. One day, my eldest son, Pino, came home from school and asked me, with a very confused look on his face, what was wrong with being Italian. It seemed that he was being teased about it at school. I was sad and angry at the idea of him having to put up with the insults that still haunted me from my childhood, and yet I could not give him a clear picture as to what it meant to be Italian, because my idea of being Italian was from my parents who had left Italy some 40 years earlier!

I felt I needed to find out for myself. I needed to experience the culture, the customs, the peculiarities and pleasures of being a contemporary Italian first hand. More importantly, I wanted my children to understand what it was to be an Italian in their own way if they were going to be proud of and totally own their heritage.

So, in 1986, my little family moved to Italy, where we lived for six months. We visited the village of my parents and toured through Italy before settling in Impruneta, a place that has been the centre of terracotta production in Italy for a thousand years. It was here that Della Robbia and Donatello had their workshops. From here came the tiles that grace the magnificent Duomo di Firenze. In this small town, on the edge of Chianti, we made a home. The children attended school and my wife and I began to understand, grow to love and become frustrated with modern Italy.

We met many wonderful people over this time, among them Beppi and Roberta Beccucci. Beppi (short for Giuseppe) is a fourth-generation salami maker. He had a *salumeria* (sausage-making factory) where they killed up to 10 pigs a day in the centre of town, until complaints from neighbours closed them down. Admittedly, I wouldn't want to sit in the piazza with a backdrop of squealing pigs. The *salumeria* of the Beccucci family is still famous for its *finocchiona* (see page 196) and *coppa di testa* (head cheese; see page 215).'

Fennel salami from Marco of San Giovanni Valdarno

Finocchiona di Marco da San Giovanni Valdarno

This salami is made from second selection meat – such as the belly, the neck and the trimmings from the prosciutto – which is a little fattier than the meat used for other salami. You need a total of 40 per cent fat for this particular style of *finocchiona*.

In Tuscany, this can be eaten as a soft, fresh meat rather than allowing it to dry out like a typical *soppressa*. This is also called a '*sbricciolone*' or 'crumbly' because it crumbles as you cut it, but with fresh crusty bread it is absolutely sensational.

second selection pork meat and fat
sea salt (30 g per 1 kg meat/fat)
Tuscan spices (2.5 g per 1 kg meat/fat; see note)
freshly ground black pepper (2.5 g per 1 kg
    meat/fat)
whole black peppercorns (3 g per 1 kg meat/fat)
fennel seeds (15 g per 1 kg meat/fat – or two-
    thirds this amount of fennel flowers)
finely chopped garlic cloves (5 cloves per
    10 kg meat/fat)
pre-soaked ox bungs (see page 190)
    (1 bung per 2.5 kg meat)

Special equipment
meat mincer
string
large safety pin
size 16 elastic netting
meat hooks

Mince the meat and fat finely, then spread out on a large, plastic-covered table and mix with the seasonings.

Following the instructions on pages 190–192, press the mince into the ox bungs, pierce the skins 10 to 20 times, then place in the netting and hang for 4 weeks or more. The salami can be eaten after 4 weeks but it will still be quite soft. You can leave it to mature and dry for a further 3 months, at which stage it should be transferred to vacuum-sealed bags.

Variation

Finocchiona di Beccucci

This is a posher version, made with lean meat and good-quality fat. Make a mixture of 60–70 per cent lean meat and 30–40 per cent good-quality fat. Mince finely. For every 1 kg of mince add 30 g of sea salt, 1.5 g of fennel seeds, 2 g of whole black peppercorns, 0.6 g of finely chopped garlic and 0.2 g of sodium nitrate (Chile saltpetre). Knead the mixture, then cover and leave overnight.

Following the instructions on pages 190, press the mince into pre-soaked ox bungs. Tie the bungs firmly every 10 cm; this keeps the large salamis firm, as well as allowing you to hang the salamis from the centre rather than the end. This helps prevent the salamis from falling.

Pierce the skins 10 to 20 times. Hang the salamis as described on pages 191–192. After 1 week, a mould will possibly form on the outside but you can simply wipe this away. After 1 month, they will be covered in mould but don't worry! After 2 months, the salamis will begin to shrink and the mould will start to turn grey. After 4 months, the mould will be thick, dry and uniform, and the *finnochiona* is now ready to eat after being wiped clean.

Note: In Italy, one can buy pre-prepared Tuscan spices. The recipe is equal parts cinnamon, cloves and nutmeg. They are very finely ground and used in a lot of Tuscan dishes.

Small salamis for sugo

Salamino da sugo

It is a misnomer to call this a *salamino* (small salami), as it is normally encased in the pig's bladder and therefore the size of a small watermelon! But even the most red-blooded Italian family can balk at at the use of a pig's bladder, so these days we tend to use large ox bungs.

Traditionally, this would be eaten with beans, turnips and radicchio. When I used to serve it to my children and they asked what it was, I would just tell them it was 'chicken'. Hearing that it had tongue and heart in it would have put them right off! But it is extremely flavoursome, especially when eaten with crusty bread and accompanied with a glass of dry white wine.

10 kg pork meat, including the leg muscles
    and lean head meat, finely minced
½ pig's tongue, finely minced
½ pig's heart, finely minced
300 g sea salt
15 g freshly ground black pepper
½ whole nutmeg, finely grated
2 litres dry red wine
175 ml rum
4 pre-soaked ox bungs (see page 190)

Special equipment
meat mincer
string
large safety pin
size 16 elastic netting
meat hooks

Spread the minced meat out flat on a large, plastic-covered table, then mix in the salt, pepper, nutmeg, wine and rum and combine thoroughly. Cover and leave overnight, by which time the mince will absorb the liquid.

The next day, follow the instructions on pages 190–192 and press the mince into the ox bungs. Pierce the skins 10 to 20 times, then hang for 2 weeks.

When ready to eat, boil gently in plenty of water for 3–4 hours, then refrigerate. The salamis will keep in the fridge for up to 1 week.

Signora Fiorentino's liver salami from Molise

Salami di fegato alla Molisana

After butchering your choice cuts, collect the pig's liver, heart, lungs and all of the bloody meat, plus some of the bloody fat. Put this all through the mincer and mix well. The ideal ratio is three-quarters liver to one-quarter meat, plus the heart and lungs.

Weigh how much mince you have, then spread it out flat on a large, plastic-covered table. Add 28–30 g of sea salt per 1 kg of mince, plus your preferred amount of chilli powder, wild fennel seeds and freshly ground black pepper. Then, for every 1 kg of mince, crush 3 garlic cloves and place in half a glass of white wine (drink the other half of it first!). Sieve the garlic and wine over the mince (through a clean tea towel, muslin or fine metal sieve) and mix everything together well.

Following the instructions on pages 190–192, press the mince into pre-soaked *cacciatore* skins and hang for 1 week. You can now cook and eat them straight away, or you can allow them to dry for a further 6–8 weeks and eat as you would any other salami.

Stuffed pork bladder

Stomach ventricina

When showing my salami to my *commare* Domenica, who comes from Abruzzi, she threw down the ultimate challenge. According to her, the best salami in Italy is this *ventricina* from Abruzzi.

You first need to remove the bladder or stomach of the pig and soak it in water, with slices of lemon and orange and some dried bay leaves, for approximately 12 hours. Then rinse again with fresh water.

You will need the pork cheeks, a piece of pork belly, and muscle from the prosciutto. Remember to have 20–30 per cent fat to 70–80 per cent meat. Use a fine grade on the mincer to mince the meat and fat. Weigh the amount of minced meat you have and add 28 g of sea salt, 14 g of sweet paprika and 14 g of chilli powder for every 1 kg of mince. You can also add wild fennel seeds, freshly ground black and white pepper, dried rosemary and finely chopped orange peel. You can also substitute Capsicum Paste (see page 122) for paprika.

Knead the mince and seasonings together, then cover and stand for 12 hours. Fill the bladder or stomach with the spiced mince and make sure that you expel all the air. Pierce the bladder with a needle. Place in elastic netting and hang as per the instructions on pages 191–192 for 3 months. Clean off any mould with oil and vinegar, then cover in salted *stucco* or pork fat (see page 202). This will slow down the drying process over the hotter months. Eat after 6 months.

Variation

Ventricina spread
Ventricina da spalmare

Make the above mixture, then mix with just enough extra-virgin olive oil to loosen. Transfer the mixture to clean jars (see steps 1–2, page 21), completely cover with olive oil and seal. Store in a cool, dark place for 3 months, then store in the fridge and enjoy spread on crusty bruschetta.

Stuffed hock salami from Emilia

Zampone Emiliano

This is traditionally eaten at Christmas.

Remove the skin from the front leg of the pig down to the foot, but leave the toenail in place. This is what you will stuff the filling into. You will need approximately 1 kg of filling, made up of one-third skin (from the back), one-third lean meat from the head (not including the ears) and one-third lean meat from the muscles of the leg with tendons. Mince finely using the mincer through 8 mm holes.

To the mince, add 30 g of sea salt, 0.7 g of sodium nitrate (Chile saltpetre), 4 g of freshly ground black pepper, 1 g of finely chopped garlic and 4 g of a mixture of equal parts ground cinnamon, mace, nutmeg and cloves.

Knead the mixture, then cover and leave to stand overnight.

Fill the prepared skin with the mince mixture and sew up securely, making an airtight seal. Place in a 100°C (fan-forced) oven for 5–6 hours until the skin goes slightly brown.

Now you can either prepare it to eat the next day or keep it for up to 1 month in the fridge. To eat, soak the stuffed hock in cold water overnight. The next day, pierce the skin 10 to 20 times with a large needle. Gently simmer the hock in water for 4–6 hours. Do not cook it too quickly as rigorous boiling may cause it to burst. By the end of cooking, the skin will be very soft and sticky, like glue. Serve the *zampone* with lentils, beans and mashed potatoes.

Capocollo

Capocollo is made from scotch fillet, the meat from the neck of the pig, from the base of the skull down the spine to approximately the fifth rib. The meat changes colour as you go down the spine, from a dark red to a lighter pink. The darker meat makes the best *capocollo*. If you prefer, you can ask a butcher to remove the *capocollo*, already trimmed and cut.

Traditionally, you would wrap the *capocollo* in the lining of the pig's abdominal cavity, which had also been salted. Then, with split canes placed lengthways, you would wrap with thick string, tightening the string every week as the strips of cane become loose and the *capocollo* dries. These days we tend to use ox bungs.

Place the meat in a plastic container, cover liberally with fine sea salt, then cover with a clean cloth. Leave to stand for 2–5 days at room temperature. The cooler it is, the longer it will take for the salt to penetrate (it will take 20 days at 4°C). Turn the meat daily so it doesn't dry out. I pride myself on making a *capocollo* that is not too salty so I only allow it to stay under salt for 2–3 days. Wash the salt off with red wine, then dry the meat well.

At this stage, the meat can be put into a pre-soaked ox bung (see page 190) without adding any further condiments. Place two layers of size 16 netting around the bung and then prick the casing 10 to 20 times with a large safety pin. Hang in a moist, cool environment.

Variations

Dino Bertolin's prize-winning capocollo

Prepare the *capocollo* as above but leave under sea salt for 5 days. Shake off the salt. Mix a little black pepper (half fine, half coarse) with 12 cloves and a cinnamon stick using a mortar and pestle; pound until reasonably fine. Rub the *capocollo* liberally with this mixture and place in the ox bung. Tie with string every 5 cm, plus four strings lengthways, then place in two layers of size 16 elastic netting. Hang with the fatter end down, then pierce the bung three or four times. You can eat it after 2 months but it's best after at least 6 months.

Cesare's capocollo

Combine 1 kg of sea salt, 15 g of white pepper, 10 g of ground coriander, 30 g of ground mace, 3 g of sodium nitrate (Chile saltpetre), 200 g of sugar and 20 g of ground nutmeg. Cover the meat with this mixture, at a rate of 40 g per 1 kg of meat. Place in a container and leave at room temperature for 5 days, agitating every second day. Wash the mixture off with red wine, dry and place in an ox bung and size 16 elastic netting. Pierce the skins, then hang for 6 months. Note: you can also use this mixture to cure pancetta.

Tuscan capocollo

The curing mixture is made up of sea salt, garlic, rosemary and sage. Mix thoroughly and cover the meat with the mixture for 3–5 days. Proceed as for Cesare's *capocollo*.

Compare Peppino's capocollo

Rub the meat with sea salt, then place in a cold brine (100 g of salt per litre of water), which has been prepared the night before. Add some fennel seeds and a little chilli powder. Allow the meat to soak for 7 days. Remove from the brine and wash in red wine. Rub liberally with chilli powder, paprika and some crushed fennel seeds. Peppino encases the meat in the lining of the abdominal cavity of a cow, which has been trimmed by the butcher, then placed under sea salt for 3 days and washed in water and lemon before use. Wrap the meat in this lining and sew up like a sock, then place in elastic netting. Pierce the skin and hang for 3–6 months before eating.

Compare Vittorio's capocollo

This recipe produces quite a salty *capocollo*. Measure 360 g of sea salt per 10 kg of meat. Add 1 tablespoon of sugar. Mix well. Place the meat in a plastic container and cover with half the salt mix. Rotate each day. After 6 days, add the rest of the salt mix and leave for a further 6 days. Remove the meat and wash off the salt mix with white wine, then dry and place in an ox bung. Place in two layers of size 16 elastic netting and hang. Pierce after 2–3 days. Leave for 6 months. You can also use this mixture to cure pancetta.

Pancetta

Pancetta is a delicious streaky bacon made from pork belly.

Dino's pancetta from Pordenone

La pancetta di Dino di Pordenone

Remove the skin and excess fat from the pancetta. Remove the eye fillet off the back, then remove the meat off the ribs, peeling it down from the back to the teats, almost to the hind leg. Trim this so that you are left with a square piece of meat that is relatively lean, with layers of meat and a small amount of fat. Butterfly the fillet lengthways. Place the square piece of meat and the butterflied fillet under a liberal amount of sea salt and leave for 24 hours. Remove and brush off the excess salt. Sprinkle the meat with more salt, as well as some ground black pepper, chilli powder, ground cloves and cinnamon. Place the eye fillet on the thinner end of the square piece of meat and then roll the whole thing up as you would a Swiss jam roll. Wrap the meat either in abdominal lining or a pre-soaked ox bung (see page 190). Sew up securely and place in a double layer of size 16 elastic netting. Pierce the casing six or seven times with a large needle and hang for 6 months.

Abruzzese recipe for pancetta

Pancetta Abruzzese

Remove the pancetta as detailed in Dino's recipe opposite. Place the square piece of meat and the butterflied fillet in a plastic container and cover liberally with fine sea salt. Leave for 5 days, turning each day so the piece on the bottom comes to the top, and vice versa. Remove the meat and wash off the salt with red wine. Sprinkle the meat liberally with crushed Dried Hot Chillies (see page 109) and sweet paprika. Place the eye fillet on the thinner end of the square piece of meat and then roll the whole thing up as you would a Swiss jam roll. Wrap the meat either in abdominal lining or a pre-soaked ox bung (see page 190). Sew up securely and place in a double layer of size 16 elastic netting. Sprinkle some chilli powder on the outside, then pierce the casing six or seven times with a large needle and hang for 6 months.

Calabrese pancetta from Reggio

Pancetta Calabrese di Reggio

This pancetta is removed from the pig with the skin on, Calabrese style, as described on page 187. The slab of meat is removed from the back below the fillet, down to just above the teats. Place the meat in a plastic container and cover with sea salt. Leave for 4 days, turning each day so everything is evenly coated. Remove the meat from the container and wash off the salt with red wine. Cover completely on both sides with crushed Dried Hot Chillies (see page 109). Not only does this taste great, but because you don't place this style of pancetta in a protective casing, the chillies also keep away the flies!

The pancetta is then hung up as a slab. Make sure you put some chilli into the hole that you make to pass the string through to hang the pancetta, as you do not want flies anywhere near the meat. This pancetta takes much less time to cure; it can be eaten after 6 weeks, but will keep for much longer. It is fantastic with fried eggs for breakfast.

Smoked pancetta

Pancetta affumicata

This pancetta recipe needs sodium nitrate (Chile saltpetre) to stop the fat becoming rancid in the smoking process. Make a mixture of 3 g of sodium nitrate, 30 g of sugar and 10 g of ground black pepper per 1 kg of sea salt. Remove as much fat as possible from the pancetta. Place in a plastic tub, cover with the salt mixture and leave for 5 days, turning each day. When ready, hang the meat in an enclosure (such as a metal locker), suspended well above the base. Buy some juniper wood sawdust or chips (or use hickory chips). Set the sawdust or chips alight and, just when they seem to be catching, stop the flame. This will produce a dense smoke. Seal the enclosure and leave the meat to hang with this smoke for 48 hours. The temperature needs to stay below 18°C, otherwise the fat will become rancid. After the smoking, hang and leave to dry for a further 3–4 weeks before eating.

Belly of pork, San Giovanni style

Tarese di San Giovanni valdarno

This pancetta is traditionally made from pigs that weigh in excess of 200 kg, with each belly of pork weighing up to 20 kg. However, the recipe can also be used for smaller cuts of pork belly and the flavour is still aromatic and overwhelmingly good. Remove the belly of pork, including the fillet, as one piece. Leave the skin on. The belly will include some ribs, which will need to be carefully boned out. Make a mixture of finely chopped rosemary and sage leaves, finely chopped garlic, freshly ground black pepper and Tuscan spices (see note, page 196). Rub this herb mixture into the cut meat. Place on a board and cover completely with sea salt. Place the board on a slight incline into a sink or container, to allow any brine that forms to drain away. The time that you leave the meat under salt will depend on the weight of the meat. If your pig is the standard 120 kg, then 5–6 days is enough. If you actually get a pig of 250 kg, then you need to allow 10 days.

After this time, wash the salt off with red wine. Make a new mixture of garlic, salt, pepper and Tuscan spices. Massage some of this into the surface of the meat, then cover the whole of the cut surface with the spice/salt mixture and hang for 2–6 months, depending on the weight of the pancetta.

Salted pork cheek

Boccolaro

This is the cheek of the pig, which is removed with as much meat as possible from the cheekbone. It is cured in exactly the same way as the Calabrese pancetta (see above), and is classically used for spaghetti alla carbonara.

Prosciutto

Prosciutto is always the pride of any serious *salumista* (salami maker) or *norcino* (specialist smallgoods butcher) and is so easy to make.

The hind leg is the first portion that is removed from the pig, before you remove the skin. Cut the hind leg and the spine off. Next, remove the prosciutto from the hip with a clean cut, making sure that you leave as much of the meat behind as possible. You obviously leave the hipbone on the prosciutto. The leg bone can be removed, but you probably need a butcher to do it for you so that it is neat and clean. In fact, it may be an idea to get a butcher to remove the prosciutto for you initially, and prepare it for you ready for salting – at least until you have seen it done once or twice.

However, if you want to do it the traditional way, continue by trimming the skin by one-third along the inside of the leg, so that you have a third of the meat exposed around the hipbone. Remove any bloody meat, particularly around the bone. Be careful not to create spaces next to the bone. Remove the trotter by cutting across with a saw. The final cut surface of the prosciutto should be unbroken and clean. The leg is then laid down on a large, steady surface with the cut surface facing upwards.

With a rolling pin, press along the bone firmly, extracting any blood left in the veins that run along the bone for the whole length of the prosciutto. Do this daily for a week or until no further blood comes out of the veins. This is tedious, sure, but essential, as any blood left in the veins along the bone will result in the meat rotting.

Once drained of all blood, the prosciutto is then laid on a bed of rock salt with the raw face upwards on a slight angle to allow any juices to drain. Cover the entire cut surface and end with a 2–3 cm thick layer of rock salt, making sure that the salt fills all the crevices, particularly around the exposed bone. It is easy at this stage to push the salt into the meat around the bone and create hollows. Avoid this if you can. Make sure you also cover the cut end of the prosciutto where the trotter was. Any exposed bone and meat can be the entry point for flies and putrefaction. Allow the meat to remain under salt for 1 day per 1 kg of meat (I find with a 120 kg pig, a week is long enough). Some recipes ask for the prosciutto to be placed under salt for 14 days. This will make the meat slightly saltier but it will also make it less likely to go rotten. If you want to use sodium nitrate (Chile saltpetre) to enhance the colour of the cut meat, add 20 g of sodium nitrate per 100 kg of meat.

After the period under salt, remove and brush off all the salt. This is important because you need the surface to become dry, and if the surface has any salt remaining it will stay moist. At this stage, again, try and express as much blood from the vein along the bone with a rolling pin. Some say to put the prosciutto under a weight of approximately 40 kg (a board with a bag of cement on top is the usual method!) for a week. This ensures that the prosciutto is firm and does not have any trapped juices, blood or cavities that can putrefy. I recommend doing this.

Wash the cut surface with red wine and dry thoroughly. Cover the entire cut surface with black or white pepper, making sure that you also cover the cut hoof. Note that this is only to deter flies. If the prosciutto is allowed to dry for too long the meat will dry out and lose its magical transparent red colour. After 2–3 months, when the surface is dry and the prosciutto is beginning to dry out, make a mixture of fresh raw pork fat, salt and flour (known as *stucco*). The consistency should be like putty. Cover the entire exposed surface with this 'putty' and then cover with white pepper again. This will slow down the drying process and keep the prosciutto moist. It will also prevent the outer layer of meat from turning black, which would then need to be discarded. The prosciutto is best if left to cure for 1 year. The ideal curing temperature is 13°C with 80 per cent humidity.

Prosciutto troubleshooting

My prosciutto has maggots crawling all over it!

This has happened because flies have got to it. Sadly, there is nothing to be done except throw it away and try again! In future, this can be avoided by covering all the exposed meat and bone ends with the salt, and by covering the prosciutto with a fly net.

My prosciutto has started rotting/has a terrible smell/has gone a grey colour

This means the meat was not fully cured with the salt and therefore it has started to putrefy. This happened because it did not have enough exposed meat and/or it was not under salt long enough and/or the blood from the veins along the bone was not expressed adequately. In future, make sure the meat is adequately and fully salted and that you place the prosciutto under a weight for a week after being salted to expel any further blood or trapped juices that can cause the meat to go off.

Boneless prosciutto

Prosciutto senza osso

A less traditional but much safer way of making prosciutto is to remove the bone (as well as the artery and vein attached to the bone). This means that there is less chance of spoilage from the blood left in the vein. It is also easier when you want to slice the prosciutto, because there is no bone to cut through.

Trim the meat to the exposed round knob on the end of the leg bone (following the general prosciutto instructions, see page 202). Trim the skin slightly. Place the leg on the bench and you will notice that the bone is closer to one edge than the other. Place the leg so that the bone is furthest away from you, then cut the skin just above the bone from the ankle to the end of the bone. Cut down the length of the bone and around it, making sure that you have removed the vein and artery, and then remove the bone and blood vessels together. You will now have a leg that is sliced open. Cover the meat surfaces and the exposed ends of the leg liberally with a mixture of rock salt and table salt. You can also add spices to the salt mix at this stage if you want. Some suggestions are:

* freshly ground black pepper (Abruzzi)
* freshly ground black pepper mixed with dried chilli flakes (Calabria)
* freshly ground black pepper mixed with finely chopped fresh garlic, rosemary and sage (Tuscany)
* white pepper, ground nutmeg, ground allspice and ground cloves mixed with salt (Tuscany)

For a 10 kg prosciutto, leave under salt for 7–8 days on a slightly inclined board (for example, a wooden chopping board on an angle in the sink) to allow drainage. Because the leg has been opened it will salt more quickly than a whole leg. Hold the prosciutto up by the ankle and shake off the excess salt. Cover the exposed surfaces with your chosen mix of spices.

Hang to dry at approximately 16°C, with a humidity of approximately 70–80 per cent. You can fold the cut meat back to recreate the shape of the leg, but if you do this, you will need to place a clamp on the leg to ensure that the cut surfaces are pressed tightly against each other.

Allow to hang for 8–12 months. You will notice that a white mould will form, mixed with the spices. This mould is normal; just cut the surface off before slicing to serve.

Smoked prosciutto

Prosciutto affumicato

Prepare the prosciutto as for Boneless Prosciutto (see opposite). When ready, hang the meat in an enclosure (such as a metal locker), suspended well above the base. You will need some moistened juniper wood sawdust or chips (or use hickory chips pre-soaked in water for 24 hours). Set the moist sawdust or chips alight and, just when they seem to be catching, stop the flame. This will produce a dense smoke. Seal the enclosure and leave the meat to hang with this smoke for 4–5 days. Because the chips are not alight, the temperature will remain very low; it needs to remain constant at 16–18°C. Repeat the smoking process 3–4 times a day for 4–5 days, then cover the prosciutto in pepper and hang it. After 3–4 months, seal it with a salt/fat mix (see page 202) and leave for another 12 months before eating.

Smoked shoulder ham/speck

Prosciutto di spalla affumicato

In the alpine region of the Dolomites, in Northern Italy, the speciality is speck or smoked *prosciutto crudo*. The basic technique is the same but the cut of meat is the shoulder. Ideally the pig is lean, so you will end up with the skin, a 1–2 cm layer of fat and the shoulder muscle. This will minimise the tendency for the fat to become rancid. Prepare the shoulder in the same way as the prosciutto on page 202.

After the salting process, it is time to smoke the meat. This can be done with green pine needles or with hickory chips; both give a distinctive flavour and are easily obtained. Traditionally, juniper wood sawdust is used but this will be harder to find. When ready, hang the meat in an enclosure (such as a metal locker), suspended well above the base. The pine needles or wood chips need to be moist so as to produce smoke and not a flame. If using hickory chips, soak them in water for 24 hours before placing them on hot coals. Seal the enclosure and leave the meat to hang with this smoke for 6–8 days, repeating the smoking process three or four times a day. The temperature needs to remain constant at no more than 16°C. After the smoking process, leave the meat to hang in the enclosure for a further 2–3 days. In the Dolomites, the meat is smoked for 15 days until it becomes black. I find that the smoky taste is overpowering if the meat is allowed to smoke for this long.

Once the speck is smoked, allow it to hang and dry as for *capocollo* or pancetta for 3–6 months. If you do not seal the meat with a salt/fat mix (see page 202), it will dry faster and so will be ready to eat earlier.

Sausages

Salsicce

The meat to make fresh sausages does not need to be as lean as for salamis, although too much fat is not ideal. A mixture of belly and shoulder meat is best.

Dino's fresh sausages

Salsicce fresche di Dino

Remove the meat from the cheeks and head of the pig and collect any scraps that are slightly fatty or bloody. Combine these with all the scraps from the pancetta and the leg to make up 15 kg of meat (you can add 3 kg of stewing steak if you need to). Mince coarsely. Add 300 g of sea salt, 30–45 g of freshly ground black pepper and 250 ml of garlic wine mix (see Venetian Salami, page 193). Add a handful of fennel seeds and some chilli powder, if you like. Following the instructions on pages 190–192, press the mince into pre-soaked lamb's bungs and eat straight away, either boiled or grilled.

Variation

Offal salami
Salame di frattaglie

This is a good way to use up any bloodied and fatty meat with tendons and sinews that is not suitable for making salamis on its own. Gather up these meat scraps. Remove the windpipe from the lungs and add to the meat scraps. Remove the kidneys, then slice and sear them on a hot grill to remove the smell of urine. Add these to the meat scraps, along with the heart and one-third of the liver. Mince coarsely, then weigh the amount of mince you have. For every 1 kg of mince, add 30 g of sea salt. Add 2.5 kg of Dino's fresh sausage mince (see above), 500 ml of wine and 20 g of freshly ground black pepper, then mix well. Following the instructions on pages 190–192, press the mince into pre-soaked fine sausage skins, then hang and eat within 2–3 weeks.

Oreste's fresh sausages

Salsicce fresche di Oreste

15 kg pork shoulder
1 garlic clove, crushed and placed in 250 ml white wine, left overnight
225 g sea salt
2 tablespoons freshly ground black pepper
1 teaspoon freshly ground nutmeg
2 teaspoons freshly ground cloves
15–20 pre-soaked lamb's bungs (see page 190)

Coarsely mince the pork and spread out flat on a large, plastic-covered table. Strain the garlic wine mix through a clean muslin bag or fine sieve, then mix the liquid into the meat. Add the salt, pepper and spices and mix thoroughly.

Following the instructions on pages 190–192, press the mince into the bungs, slightly loose, and allow to rest overnight. The next day, the sausages are ready to cook or grill on the barbecue, or you can freeze them for 2–3 months.

Variation

Fresh sausages from Lucca
Salsicce fresche Lucchesi

Follow the recipe above, but omit the pepper and add ground cinnamon and allspice. Make the sausages as above, 10 cm long.

Liver sausages

Salsicce di fegato

For these sausages, you can use either a range of organs – including the liver, heart and lungs – or a mixture of liver and meat. There are several variations.

Recipe 1

Coarsely mince the liver, heart and lungs. Weigh the amount of mince you have. Add 30 g of sea salt for every 1 kg of mince, plus your desired amount of freshly ground black pepper and fennel seeds. Mix well and press the mince into pre-soaked thin sausage skins. Hang to dry for 3–4 weeks, then place under oil or *sugna* (melted pork fat), where they will keep for 2–3 months.

Recipe 2

Mix the pork liver with an equal amount of lean pork meat. Mince coarsely, then add small cubes of pork fat from the back of the pig. Mix well. Weigh the amount of mince you have. Add 30 g of sea salt for every 1 kg of mince, plus your desired amount of fennel seeds and freshly ground black pepper. Mix well and press into pre-soaked thin sausage skins. Hang to dry in a moist place for 3–4 weeks, then place under pork fat as above or freeze for 2–3 months. These sausages can also be cooked fresh but, if doing so, you only need to use 15 g of sea salt per 1 kg of meat. You can't hang them to dry with only 15 g of salt as they will go off very quickly.

Recipe 3

Coarsely mince the liver and heart, 500 g of fat from the back of the pig and 500 g of lean meat. Add 3–4 very finely chopped garlic cloves and some chilli powder. This actually adds a nice flavour, so be brave and don't omit it! Add 30 g of sea salt per 1 kg of mince and the grated zest of 1 orange. Mix well and press into pre-soaked *cacciatore* skins. If you want to cook these sausages fresh, add only 15 g of salt per 1 kg of mince, then cook straight away or freeze. If hanging them to dry, allow 3–5 weeks to dry before placing under oil or *sugna* (pork fat). They can also be frozen for 2–3 months after hanging.

Enzo and Tina's liver sausages

Salsicce di fegato di Enzo e Tina

This is the best recipe – but don't quote me on that, because I will deny that I ever said it about an Abruzzese!

Ask the butcher for a 'pluck' of pork. This is the heart, lungs and liver in one piece. Remove the trachea, slice the heart open and remove the blood. Weigh the offal and add the same weight in pork shoulder meat (include some fat, but remove the skin). Coarsely mince the offal and meat.

Weigh the amount of mince you have, then for every 1 kg of mince, add 28 g of sea salt and 4 g of dried chilli flakes, plus 6 large cloves of garlic, finely chopped. Mix well and allow to stand overnight. Test by frying a small amount and tasting to see if it has enough salt and chilli for your liking.

Following the instructions on pages 190–192, press the mince into pre-soaked small sausage skins and hang for 4–5 weeks. Do not allow the sausages to become too hard. After hanging, place in vacuum-sealed bags and store in the fridge for up to 3 months. This sausage is slightly soft but delicious.

Maria Luisa and Gabriella's terrine sausage from Le Marche

Il ciauscolo Marchiggiano di Maria Luisa e Gabriella

Il ciauscolo is unique to the Marche region. Its smooth, creamy consistency allows it to be spread over bread rather than eaten in slices. This recipe was given to me by Maria Luisa, a very dear friend who died in 2004. She was a treasured, dynamic, loving and dedicated woman. This is the recipe as once made by her family in Borgiano and still currently produced in the region of Le Marche. When you are sitting having a crostini with this delicious spread, send a quiet *grazie* to our dear friend.

1 garlic clove, crushed
splash of white wine
1 kg lean pork shoulder
800 g pancetta (fattier than shoulder)
28 g sea salt
4 g freshly ground black pepper
pinch of ground nutmeg
1 pre-soaked ox bung (see page 190)

Special equipment
meat mincer
string
large safety pin
size 16 elastic netting
meat hooks

Add the crushed garlic to the wine and allow the mixture to stand for several hours. Strain and discard the garlic. Mince all the ingredients together, running through the mincer three times, each time more finely. This is very important as it produces a smooth, creamy consistency, which is the main characteristic of the *ciauscolo*.

Following the instructions on pages 190–192, press the mince into the ox bung, pierce a few times with a pin and place in the elastic netting, then hang for a minimum of 3 months. Enjoy spread over crusty bread.

Signora Fiorentino's soppressate from Molise

Soppressate alla Molisana di Signora Fiorentino

Soppressate are large sausages that have been weighed down during the drying process, resulting in a flattish shape.

For every 1 kg of lean pork meat, use 10 g of fine back fat, 30 g of sea salt and 1 teaspoon of whole black peppercorns.

Mince the meat very finely, then cut the fat into 1 cm cubes and mix with the other ingredients on a large, plastic-covered table. Following the instructions on pages 190–192, press the mince into pre-soaked lamb's bungs and hang for 5–6 days, then place under a heavy weight (say 10 kg) until the *soppressate* acquire a squashed look.

Hang for 3 months. Traditionally, they are then placed under olive oil to stop them from drying further (see page 192). When you want to eat them, remove them from the oil, peel off the skins and slice.

Cotechino

When Italians take the trouble to source or rear an organic pig, nothing is wasted!

Collect all the gristle from the butchering – the tendons, the meat from the face, the glands around the neck. Mix with equal quantities of skin that has had all the fat removed (the best is from the back and the thigh rather than the abdomen). For every 12 kg of gristle mix, add 7 kg of gravy beef (in Italy, horse meat might be added). Pass this mixture twice through the mincer.

For every 1 kg of mince, add 30 g of sea salt, 2 g of black pepper (a mixture of ground and whole) and the remaining 500 ml of garlic wine mix left over from making the Venetian Salami (see page 193). Following the instructions on pages 190–192, press into pre-soaked lamb's bungs and hang for approximately 1 month.

You need to cook these before eating them. Simply boil for about 1 hour, then slice. *Cotechino* is traditionally eaten with beans, pickled cabbage and pickled turnips (see page 242).

Variations

Cotechino from Bologna
Cotechino di Bologna

Make the meat mixture as above but add 1.5 g of sodium nitrate (Chile saltpetre) and 1.5 g of ground nutmeg for every 1 kg of mix.

Tongue salami
Linguale

This special salami is used to break the fast at Easter in Veneto. Clean the pig's tongue and slice down the centre. Place in a plastic container, cover with fine sea salt and stand for 12 hours. Wash off the excess salt with white wine and sprinkle with freshly ground black pepper. Close the tongue and place in a pre-soaked ox bung. Surround the tongue with *cotechino* mince so as to create a sausage that has *cotechino* on the outside and tongue on the inside. Tie with four strings to keep firm. Allow to hang for 3–4 months before eating. To eat, boil for 1 hour, then slice and serve as you would *cotechino*.

Other cured meat recipes

Salt-cured beef

Bresaola

Bresaola is made from beef or, in Italy, sometimes horse meat. The important thing is that the meat has not been frozen and is of the best quality. Normally the cuts used are the *girello*, the fillet or the rump. Ensure that there are no tendons or hard white fibres in the meat.

4 litres red wine
1 kg coarse sea salt
12 rosemary sprigs
1 bunch of thyme
2 large white onions, roughly chopped
8 large garlic cloves, crushed
125 g freshly ground black pepper
125 g juniper berries, crushed
1 tablespoon dried chilli flakes
peel of 2 oranges, cut into large pieces
5 kg beef topside, trimmed of all fat

Special equipment
meat hooks

Place all the ingredients, apart from the beef, in a large container and mix well to make a marinade. Place the meat in the marinade, ensuring that it is well covered, then cover and leave to marinate in the fridge or a cool cellar for 1 week. Remove and pat dry, then hang in a cool place for 3 weeks, or until the meat feels firm. When ready, it may have developed a white mould. Wash this off with vinegar, pat dry and rub all over with olive oil. Wrap in baking paper and place in the fridge. You can also store it in vacuum-sealed bags.

Serve the *bresaola* very finely sliced with rocket, olive oil and shaved parmesan. It can also be served with quartered figs. Alternatively, you can crisp some slices of *bresaola* in a pan as you would bacon, then break into pieces and scatter over a salad of spinach, radicchio and pine nuts dressed with olive oil and balsamic vinegar.

Cured goat

Mocetta

This is a traditional cured meat from Valle D'Aosta made with wild goat's meat.

3 large garlic cloves, crushed
1 bunch of flat-leaf parsley, chopped
1 rosemary sprig, leaves picked and chopped
200 g coarse sea salt, plus extra to layer
1 thyme sprig, leaves picked
a few juniper berries, crushed
1 teaspoon whole black peppercorns, crushed
5 kg lean mountain goat, cut into 1 kg pieces

Special equipment
10 kg weight (about 4 bricks are ideal)
meat hooks

Combine all the ingredients, apart from the goat, in a bowl. In a large container, place a layer of salt at the bottom, then arrange the meat in layers, with the garlic/herb/salt mixture in between. Cover the meat with a plate or wooden tray and place a 10 kg weight on top. Leave for 8 days in a cool spot, checking each day. Remove any liquid as it forms. Shake the meat free of excess salt and then hang in a cool, dry, well-ventilated spot for 1 month.

Serve in very thin slices with boiled potatoes and fresh bread.

Salted topside

Bresaola

This classic recipe from Emilia-Romagna is a variation on *bresaola*.

225 g sea salt
12 garlic cloves
10 dried bay leaves
2 rosemary sprigs
2 tablespoons dried marjoram
10 g whole black peppercorns
20 juniper berries
5 kg beef topside

Special equipment
10 kg weight (about 4 bricks is ideal)
cellulose sheet
size 16 elastic netting
meat hooks

Mix the salt, garlic, herbs and spices together well, then massage into the topside. Cover the meat with a plate or wooden tray and place a 10 kg weight on top. Place in the fridge and rotate each day for 10 days. It will lose approximately 20 per cent of its weight.

Wrap in a cellulose sheet and place in a large elastic netting (both of these things are available from your butcher). Hang for approximately 1 month before vacuum sealing or slicing to eat straight away as part of an antipasto.

Calabrese 'nduja

'Nduja di Calabria

This is made from all the offcuts of the pig. Usually it is the larger pigs (older than 14 months) that are used, and mainly the fatty bits left over from the salami making. As a rough guide, you need 25 per cent meat (the *guanciale* or pork cheeks and pancetta), 65 per cent fat (preferably the nicer firm fat) and 10 per cent skin.

Beware – this stuff is hot. If you don't want it so hot, you can add less chilli, but then ... it's not quite the real thing.

Cut the meat, fat and skin very finely (or finely mince). Weigh how much you have, then add 250 g of finely chopped Dried Hot Chillies (see page 109) and 20 g of sea salt per 1 kg of fatty cut meat. Note that this is less than the usual minimum of salt required to preserve salamis, but the chilli acts as a preservative* and has an antioxidant effect of its own, so you do not need as much salt as you normally would. Mix everything until well combined.

Following the instructions on pages 190–192, press the mixture into lamb's bungs and hang for up to 1 year in a slow-drying environment. When you want to eat it, remove the skin and use as a spread.

'Nduja can be used in pasta, as a flavouring, or as a spread on freshly toasted bruschetta. It is a surprisingly delectable spread with a lingering effect ... much like any full-blooded Calabrese boy!

Variation

This recipe for *'nduja* comes from the butcher in Varapodio. Use the same mixture of meat, fat and skin as opposite but boil the skin first until it is soft, then chop. To prepare the chilli, chop the dried chillies, remove the seeds and mix with a small amount of water. Simmer gently until you have a soft paste-like consistency. For every 5 kg of meat/fat/skin mixture add 140 g of sea salt and 1 kg of Hot Chilli Paste (see page 122). Mix well. Put the mixture through the mincer on a fine setting (you can do it twice if you like it extra fine). Following the instructions on pages 190–192, press the mixture into pre-soaked lamb's bungs. Hang to dry for 4–6 weeks, at which point it will be ready to eat as a spread on crusty bread.

*Tongue-in-cheek note: We are looking at developing a Calabrian embalming system where you lay the body in chilli powder for a month. It may need some more work but we will eventually get it right.

Pig's head in aspic (presswurst, Italian style)

Coppa di testa

You may be a little put off by the title of this recipe, but don't be. This is a fantastic cold meat, delicious when eaten with a nice fresh salsa verde.

As always, it is hard to give exact quantities as it depends on the weight of the meat you have. Make sure you weigh it so you can add the other ingredients accurately.

Recipe 1
Beccucci's

Cut the pig's head into pieces but try to keep the tongue whole. Place in a large stockpot and cover with water. Boil the head until the meat easily comes off the bone (which will take approximately 2 hours). Reserve the cooking water. Shred the meat off the bone and cut up into large pieces. Weigh the meat.

For every 1 kg of meat, add 33 g of sea salt, 0.2 g of sodium nitrate (Chile saltpetre), 3.5 g of freshly ground black pepper, 3.5 g of lemon juice, 2 g of grated garlic, 5 g of sugar, 1 g of ground nutmeg, 1 g of ground cinnamon and 0.5 g of ground cloves. Place the meat and seasonings in a wide-necked ceramic bowl, mix and cover with some of the reserved cooking water. Place a plate on top, then a weight, and leave in the fridge overnight for the meat to press and the liquid to set to jelly; it is then ready to eat. This will keep for 1–2 weeks in the fridge.

Recipe 2

Place the pig's head in a large stockpot and cover with water. Add salt to taste, as if you were preparing to cook pasta, plus 2–3 dried bay leaves. Boil for 2–3 hours, until the meat is ready to fall off the bone. Remove the meat (reserving the cooking water), cut coarsely and place in a large bowl. Add some freshly ground black pepper and cover with some of the reserved cooking water. Place a plate on top, then a weight, and leave in the fridge overnight. As it cools it will form a mould of meat and gelatine, which is delicious eaten with fresh bread. This will keep for 1–2 weeks in the fridge.

Recipe 3
From Marco, a butcher in
San Giovanni Valdarno

Boil the pig's head, together with 2 kg of cleaned skin and 5 pigs' tongues, for 3 hours or until the meat falls off the bone. Place the meat in a bowl and add 2 finely chopped garlic cloves, the grated zest of 4 oranges and 3 lemons, and a bunch of finely chopped flat-leaf parsley, together with sea salt (25 g per 1 kg of meat), freshly ground black pepper (2.5 g per 1 kg) and Tuscan spices (2 g per 1 kg; see note page 196). Mix thoroughly, then place in a clean linen sack and allow to hang until it firms up. The extra tongues produce a firmer consistency and leaner end result. Store in the fridge, where it can be eaten after 1 day. It will keep for 1–2 weeks in the fridge.

Signora Giovanna's pig's head in aspic

U sudzu gelatina di Signora Giovanna

This recipe, supplied by Signora Giovanna, comes from Catanzaro, where they *do* actually make the best *sudzu*. You may be surprised at how simple the recipe is. When I asked whether you add pepper or chilli, Signora Giovanna said, 'No, because young children may not like the pepper!'. I can't imagine the average six- or seven-year-old eating pig's head in aspic, but who knows?

1 pig's head
4 pig's trotters
1 kg lean pork meat, roughly cut
white wine vinegar
sea salt

Place the pig's head, trotters and meat in a large stockpot and cover with water. Bring to the boil. When the water comes to the boil, it will form a thick, frothy scum. Remove this with a slotted spoon and discard. Reduce the heat and simmer for approximately 2 hours or until the meat falls off the bones. Drain off the liquid and set aside for later. Remove as many of the bones as you can from the meat, then discard the bones, and set the meat aside.

Measure the amount of reserved liquid you have, then return it to the stockpot and add half the volume in white wine vinegar, plus enough salt to taste (as you would for cooking pasta). Return the meat to the liquid and bring to the boil again. Remove the meat with a slotted spoon and place in clean jars (see steps 1–2, page 21), then cover with the hot cooking liquid, leaving a 2 cm gap at the top of the jars if you are going to seal them hermetically. Make sure that you also allow a little of the clear liquid fat to settle on top of the meat in the jars.

If you are going to eat the *sudzu* soon, place it straight in the fridge. However, you can keep it for months by hermetically sealing the jars (see page 21) in a hot water bath for 20 minutes, then storing them in a cool, dark place. Once opened, the *sudzu* will keep in the fridge for 1–2 weeks.

Black puddings

Sanguinaccio

The very first thing that you need for *sanguinaccio* is blood!

I remember visiting my friend Renato in Pordenone on the day after Christmas. At dawn, from every farmyard in the district, you could hear the squealing of pigs destined for salami. At Renato's farm, the cauldron was boiling and the cow pen, a makeshift abattoir for the day, was filled with smoke. The frost was crunchy and thick outside, and we were freezing, waiting for the great moment. There was a strange scent in the air – of herbs and burnt skin and hair. Then in walked Zio Giorgio with the prize pig and all the instruments of torture. After the fatal blow (to the pig), Zio Giorgio plunged a knife into the pig's neck and out flowed the blood. Zia Nives was ready with the bowl and whisk. As the blood collected into the bowl, she whisked it briskly to prevent it from clotting. After about 10 minutes of whisking, she was able to stop without the blood setting. It was then taken quickly into the stone kitchen, where the *sanguinaccio* was made.

These days, you can just ask the butcher to collect the blood for you!

There are many variations of black pudding – and in Italy, it's not quite the same as the Australian/British black puddings. We have sweet versions of it too.

217

Gina's black pudding from Abruzzi

Sanguinaccio Abruzzese di Gina

5 litres pig's blood
100 g sultanas
grated zest of 1 orange
400 g fresh white breadcrumbs
250 g pork fat, cut into small cubes
110 g sea salt
pre-soaked *cacciatore* skins (see page 190)

Combine all the ingredients (apart from the *cacciatore* skins) in a large mixing bowl. Once combined, follow the instructions on pages 190–192 and press the mixture into *cacciatore* skins, but only fill them halfway (if overfilled they will burst). Place the half-filled *cacciatore* in a large stockpot of warm water and gradually bring to almost boiling point, until the sausages float to the surface. Plunge the sausages into cold water to set, then store in the fridge for up to 2 weeks. They can be cooked and eaten straight away.

Beccucci's black pudding

Buristo di Beccucci

For this black pudding, you will need a mixture of one-third pig's blood, one-third pig skin and one-third pork fat. The skin is boiled for 20 minutes, then finely minced in a meat mincer through 4 mm holes. The fat is cut into small cubes (approximately 1 cm). Mix the blood, skin and fat with 35 g of sea salt per 1 kg of meat, 35 g of breadcrumbs, 4 g of sultanas/raisins and 4 g of pine nuts. Following the instructions on pages 190–192, press the mixture into pre-soaked *cacciatore* skins, filling only to one-third capacity (if overfilled they will burst). Puncture the skins and simmer on a very low heat for 3 hours. Once cooked, pierce the skins again. These will keep in the fridge for up to 6 months and can be cooked and eaten straight away.

Cesare's black pudding from the north-east

Sanguinaccio di Cesare dal nord est

For this black pudding, you will need 5 litres of pig's blood and 110 g of sea salt. Fry up 2 chopped onions, 4 chopped garlic cloves and 1 teaspoon each of dried oregano and sage in some butter. Add the salt. You can also add cooked pork skin, cooked meat that has been cut into small cubes, or small cubes of fat. Place the fried onion mixture in a clean muslin bag and drain off the liquid, then combine the onion mixture with the blood. Following the instructions on pages 190–192, press the mixture into pre-soaked *cacciatore* skins (only fill to two-thirds capacity or they will burst when cooked). Tie the sausages into a circle with the two tied ends together. Lower into a stockpot of water approximately 80°C in temperature and gradually bring the water to just under boiling point (approximately 85°C). When the sausages are cooked, they will float to the surface. Immediately plunge them into cold water and leave for 1 hour. This will set the sausages. Store them in the fridge for up to 2 weeks. They can be cooked and eaten straight away.

Connie's black pudding, Nutella style

Sanguinaccio dolce di Connie

This is used as a sweet spread (similar to Nutella). Try it and see!

1 litre pig's blood
3 litres *Mosto Cotto* (page 239) or marsala
250 g salted butter, melted
1.5 kg ground almonds
grated zest of 1 orange
grated zest of 1 lemon
3 tablespoons ground cinnamon
500 g dark cooking chocolate
60 g cocoa powder
up to 250 g savoiardi (sponge finger biscuits), crumbled (if needed)

Combine the pig's blood, *mosto cotto* or marsala and melted butter in a large saucepan over low heat. Add the remaining ingredients, except for the savoiardi, stirring constantly. Cook over low heat for 3 hours, stirring frequently. When it is cooked, it will be a dark colour and will not run when tested on a cold spoon (similar to jam). If it does not thicken, you can add up to 250 g of crumbled savoiardi. While still hot, follow the instructions on page 21 and pour into clean jars, leaving a 2 cm gap at the top of the jars. Screw on the lids, then seal hermetically in a hot water bath for 20 minutes to ensure they are airtight. The *sanguinaccio* is ready to eat straight away. Store in a cool, dark place for up to 1 year unopened. Once opened, it will keep in the fridge for up to 2 weeks.

Black pudding from Catanzaro

Sanguinaccio dolce di Catanzaro

This is Calabrian Nutella!

1 litre pig's blood
1 litre *Mosto Cotto* (page 239)
500 g mixed nuts, ground
500 g dried grapes
1–2 cinnamon sticks
1–2 tablespoons cocoa powder (optional)

In a saucepan over low heat, combine all the ingredients and bring to a slow simmer. Continue simmering for approximately 1 hour, stirring frequently. Following the instructions on page 21, pour into clean jars while still hot, leaving a 2 cm gap at the top of the jars. Screw on the lids, then seal hermetically in a hot water bath for 20 minutes to ensure they are airtight. The *sanguinaccio* is ready to eat straight away. Store in a cool, dark place for up to 1 year unopened. Once opened, it will keep in the fridge for up to 2 weeks.

Pig's head with pork blood

Coppa e sangue

Make the *Coppa di Testa* recipe on page 215, but do not throw out the liquid you've cooked the head in. Mix the spiced meat with the pig's blood that you have collected and whisked. Following the instructions on pages 190–192, press into pre-soaked ox bungs, but only fill them by two-thirds or they may burst when you cook them. Tie securely and place the filled bungs in the reserved head-poaching liquid. Boil for 20 minutes on a low heat, then remove and cool. The sausages will keep in the fridge for 2–3 days.

Soap

Sapone

Truly, nothing is wasted when you kill a pig – it is a creature of so many uses. You can even make soap!

During the war, my mother used to take her daily laundry to the stream in a wicker basket on her head with a large piece of homemade soap. She would spend an hour washing with many other women, in between working in the fields and serving up meals. They would sing traditional Calabrian folk songs while they beat the clothes on the rocks, smoothed with years of use, and then rub them with ashes. The lime in the ashes would act as bleach. Lastly, the clothes would be washed with the dark homemade soap.

My mother had sheets that she had spun herself from raw cotton as a young girl, which were put aside as part of her dowry. They would literally last a lifetime. The sheets were heavy and coarse, with little knots through them. After washing, they were laid out in the sun to give them a freshness that was as unique as the sheets themselves. My mother and many of her *commare* always maintained that the only soap worth using on clothes is homemade soap.

Homemade soap
Sapone fatto a casa

Always wear gloves when you're making soap and immediately wash off any liquid that comes into contact with your skin.

You will need the leftover fat from the pig or – if you have no suitable fat left – vegetable oil. Make sure the fat has no blood or bones. Fat taken from the abdomen works best.

For every 6 kg of fat, you will need 1 kg of sodium hydroxide (NaOH) or caustic soda.

Over a very low fire, melt the fat in a large cauldron. Dissolve the caustic soda by adding it slowly to 16 litres of water (never reverse the process by adding water to caustic soda as it will spit). Once dissolved, slowly add the caustic soda solution to the hot melted fat, mixing thoroughly. Continue stirring for 30 minutes.

When the soap is ready, it will float to the top like honey. Turn off the heat and allow to cool for 2–3 days. The soap will harden on top of the now dark caustic soda. Cut the soap into 15 cm blocks and place in a draughty place to dry, at which point they can be used immediately.

WINE AND LIQUEURS

VINI E LIQUORI

11

Legend has it that the process of winemaking was discovered by an Assyrian queen. Her husband had died and, in a moment of desperation, she drank some grape juice that had fermented, assuming it would be poisonous as it had 'spoiled'. In fact, the fermented juice made her so happy that she forgot all about her troubles. Since then, countless people have used fermented grape juice to the same effect!

I have clear memories of Dad and my brothers arriving home from the Queen Victoria Market with the truck laden with grapes for the annual winemaking. They would set up a platform of corrugated iron sheets and tip the grapes onto it, one box at a time. Mum, my cousins and I would then crush the grapes with our feet, sliding all over the metal sheet, with grape pips getting caught between our toes. The rich, sweet grape juice stained our feet for a week and no amount of scrubbing could get it off.

The juice would then sit in open vats for several days before being pressed through an ancient wine press that took two adults to turn. The vinegar fly was everywhere and everything one touched had the sticky stain of grape juice, but finally the barrels were sealed. One year, for some unknown reason, the barrels were sealed a little early while the fermentation was still happening. The next morning, we were greeted with the sound of multiple explosions. Coursing down the garage floor, under the door and onto the footpath outside were more than 300 litres of wine. The pressure created by the wine fermenting had exploded the barrels! We never made that mistake again.

Once the wine barrels were opened in September, Dad would transfer the wine to half-gallon glass containers. He would only ever drink about a third of what he produced each year, because his greatest pleasure was making sure that anyone who came to the door would always leave with a container of his wine under their arm.

The only problem was that once the wine was placed in the containers, we had to drink it quickly before it oxidised and turned into vinegar! The only time we drank Coca Cola as a family was to add it to the wine in increasing proportions, as the wine became more and more undrinkable. In the end, we would be drinking three parts Coke and one part wine!

These days, it is possible to be a little more sophisticated and scientific about winemaking at home, and produce some very good-quality wines.

For a start, you can buy good winemaking grapes from the best areas of South Australia or Victoria. The common red wine varieties are shiraz, cabernet sauvignon, pinot noir and grenache. The common white grapes are sauvignon blanc, chardonnay or riesling. I personally find that the best white to make at home is sauvignon blanc. It makes a fruity, crisp homemade wine. I must admit that I am not a wine connoisseur, but I like to make my own 'drinkable' wine in the traditional style.

In Europe, traditional winemaking is very popular and the process is simply to crush the grapes, squeeze the juice and allow the fermentation to give you a delectable regional wine.

In Australia, however, many home winemakers have tried the same technique with less than successful results. The main reasons that backyard wine ends up less than ideal are the wild yeast on the grape skins, the lack of scrupulous cleanliness and sterilisation, oxidation of the wine and the secondary fermentation due to oxygen, resulting in vinegar. The grape juice needs yeast to ferment, but the wild yeast that lives on grape skins in Australia is not as good as traditional European wine yeast, and will lead to a variable product each year, with no predictable outcome. So to make a good, consistent homemade wine in Australia, we have to modify the traditional techniques slightly.

My dear friend Phil Kerney, an award-winning winemaker, helped me assemble the winemaking section of this book. Thanks to Phil, you (and I) can rest assured that we will be making wine that does not need to be drunk with cola!

Steps for winemaking

You will need:

* good-quality red or white wine grapes (see below)
* a grape-crushing machine (de-stemmer)
* a large plastic vat (approximately 200 litres) with a lid for fermeting the grapes (fermenting grapes in wooden containers can lead to bacterial contamination, and copper and iron will lead to quickened oxidation)
* headboards (planks of wood or plastic cut to exactly fit the 200 litre plastic vat you are using)
* a wine press
* wine barrels (stainless steel or oak)
* barrel seals with air locks
* a number of 10 litre containers (plastic, stainless steel or demijohns)
* sodium metabisulfite (to sterilise all utensils and containers)
* potassium metabisulfite
* Campden tablets or Tannisol tablets
* a pH meter or litmus paper
* a hydrometer
* tartaric acid
* appropriate wine yeast and yeast nutrient
* pectinase enzyme
* malolactic bacteria culture
* clearing agent (bentonite)
* plenty of olives, bread and last year's wine to share with your friends while you make the wine!

The grapes need to be as fresh as possible, not mouldy or damaged. The ideal sugar content varies, depending on whether you're making red or white wine, and whether you want any residual sugar or not. If you have a hydrometer, choose grapes that show an alcohol potential of 12–14 baume for white, and 12–16 for red. You will produce approximately 13.5 litres of wine per large case of grapes (which is roughly 20 kg of white wine grapes and 16 kg of red wine grapes, but check with the grower as the volume of the cases can vary).

Preparation

The first step to making a good homemade wine is to ensure that all your supplies and ingredients are fresh and available. Begin by talking to someone at a comprehensive wine supplies store, preferably someone who runs classes and is aware of seasonal needs. Begin the preparation at least a week before you buy the grapes.

Clean and sterilise everything that will come into contact with the grapes and wine. Make sure that you only use plastic or stainless-steel utensils and that these are well maintained. If you have any rust on your grape-crushing machine you will need to clean it off and apply fresh paint. Any contact that the grape juice or wine has with reactive metals, such as copper, will begin the oxidation of the wine and alter the finished product.

To clean your utensils, use sodium metabisulfite at a rate of 25 g (or 2 tablespoons) per 1 litre of cold water. Wash and soak everything with this solution, then rinse. Be very, very careful with this chemical as it produces fumes, so ensure you are in a well-ventilated area. If you are sterilising wooden barrels, soak them with the sterilising solution and then seal. If they leak, leave them for a few days until the wood expands and the leaking stops. Before pouring the wine into the barrels, drain the liquid out and rinse thoroughly with hot water. If you do not use the barrels immediately, you will need to change the solution every 3 months.

Red wine

Prepare the containers and utensils following the instructions on page 229. You will need:

* a grape-crushing machine (de-stemmer)
* 180 kg red wine grapes
* a 200 litre plastic vat with a lid
* potassium metabisulfite
* a pH meter or litmus paper
* tartaric acid
* a hydrometer
* 1 sachet pectinase enzyme
* headboards (planks of wood or plastic cut to exactly fit the 200 litre plastic vat you are using)
* yeast nutrient (diammonium phosphate/DAP)
* good-quality red wine yeast*
* a wine press
* 2 sets of 120 litre wine barrels (either stainless steel or wood for an oak flavour), or multiple smaller barrels to make up 240 litres
* barrel seals with air locks
* multiple 10 litre containers (plastic, stainless steel or demijohns)
* malolactic bacteria culture
* Campden tablets or Tannisol tablets (optional)
* bentonite

*Every variety of grape has a specific yeast that will bring out its best qualities. Discuss with your supplier which is the best yeast for you to use.

DAY 1

Use the grape-crushing machine (de-stemmer) to crush the grapes into the large, open plastic vat.

De-stem and remove the stalks from the crushed grapes for best results (the newer grape-crushing machines will do this for you during the crushing process).

Measure how much grape juice you now have in the vat. In a glass of water, dissolve 12 g of potassium metabisulfite per 100 litres of juice. Add to the vat and mix well. This will kill the wild yeast. Take a sample of the juice and test for acid with a pH meter or litmus paper. The pH should be 3.2–3.5. If higher than 3.4, add tartaric acid at a rate of 50 g for every 0.1 pH above 3.4 (so if the pH is 3.6, add 100 g of tartaric acid per 100 litres of juice). Dissolve the tartaric acid in a little juice and stir well before adding to the vat.

Test the juice with the hydrometer. The reading should be 12–14 baume. Sprinkle the sachet of pectinase enzyme over the juice, mix well and leave for 12 hours. The enzyme will help prevent a haze in the wine by breaking down proteins.

After 12 hours, apply the headboards. These allow you to press the skins down under the juice, which stops the skins floating to the surface and prevents oxidation. It also ensures that the fermentation is in contact with the skins at all times. If you do not use headboards, you will have to press the skins down manually at least twice a day using your hands or feet!

DAY 2

Remove the headboards. Dissolve a sachet of yeast nutrient (known as diammonium phosphate or DAP) in a little of the juice (you will need 12.5 g of DAP per 100 litres of juice), then add to the vat and mix well. Measure out 25 g per 100 litres of a good-quality red wine yeast and add to 10 times its weight of 37°C water. Leave for 15–20 minutes to re-hydrate, then stir gently and leave for another 5 minutes before adding to the vat and stirring in well. Apply the headboards. Cover the vat with the lid to prevent the entry of vinegar fly (a tiny fly that always seems to know when you are about to make wine).

DAY 3

By now the fermentation process will have begun and your back garden will start to smell like a winery. Your neighbours may begin to enquire as to what is happening!

DAYS 8–14

It is time to press the juice when the baume is reading below zero on a hydrometer and the colour is satisfactory. This usually takes 8–14 days but will depend on the temperature. The ideal temperature is 20–25°C. If you want a lighter-style table wine, you can press when the baume reading is between 3 and 4.

Press the fermenting juice in a wine press to separate the juice, or rather the embryonic classic vintage wine, from the skins. If you have more than one barrel, to balance the flavour out, make sure that you add the same amount of 'free running' juice and pressed juice, which will be darker and will have a higher tannin and flavour, to each barrel. Fill the barrel/s to no more than 4 cm from the top, then fit the air locks. Transfer the excess pressed juice to the 10 litre plastic or stainless-steel containers (or demijohns), as you will need this to top up the barrel/s later.

Test the wine pH – ideally you want a reading between 3.4 and 3.5. If it is higher than this, add tartaric acid at a rate of 25 g per 0.1 pH above 3.5.

While the wine is still warm, rehydrate 2.5 g of malolactic bacteria culture in five times its weight of 20°C water for every 100 litres of pressed juice. Wait 15 minutes, then add proportionally to each barrel. Keep topping up the barrel/s with the excess pressed juice from the 10 litre containers as the fermentation settles and the bubbles in the air lock cease. Air will spoil the wine, so be diligent about this.

When fermentation is complete, the wine will

* be at a baume of zero or below
* have no further bubbles forming
* not taste sweet.

When this has happened, leave the wine for 2 weeks in a cool place before moving to the next step.

DAYS 22–28

Again, test for pH and adjust if necessary as above. Now you are ready to rack the wine into a fresh, sterilised 120 litre barrel or barrels (either stainless steel or wood for an oak flavour; see page 229). For every 100 litres of wine, add 25 Campden tablets, one crushed Tannisol tablet or 12 g of potassium metabisulfite. Place this in the barrel/s into which you are racking the wine. Make sure you leave all the sediment behind when transferring from the original barrel/s.

Make sure the new barrel or barrels are as full as possible, to prevent oxidation. If you have a wooden barrel, you will need to top up with excess pressed juice every 2 weeks (or you can fit it with an 'ullage' bag to do it for you). A further racking (as above) is ideal after another 3 months to produce a cleaner flavour (so you will need to clean and re-sterilise your original barrel/s again). At the second racking, you can add bentonite at a rate of 30 g per 100 litres to encourage the suspended impurities in the wine to settle. A traditional method is to mix a whipped egg white into the wine to clear it of impurities! Each time you rack the wine, add the Campden tablets, Tannisol tablet or potassium metabisulfite at a rate of 5 g per 100 litres of wine.

Bottle the wine after 6 months, seal with corks and allow the bottles to stand upright for 1–2 weeks before drinking or cellaring. This allows any excess pressure to dissipate.

White wine

Prepare the containers and utensils following the instructions on page 229. You will need:

* 180 kg white wine grapes
* a grape-crushing machine (de-stemmer)
* a 200 litre plastic vat with a lid
* potassium metabisulfite
* a wine press
* 2 sets of stainless-steel containers (each set to make up approximately 120 litres)
* multiple 10 litre containers (plastic, stainless steel or demijohns)
* a pH meter or litmus paper
* tartaric acid
* a hydrometer
* 1 sachet Enzym Cultivar
* yeast nutrient (diammonium phosphate/DAP)
* good-quality white wine yeast*
* barrel seals with air locks
* bentonite
* Campden tablets or Tannisol tablets (optional)

*Every variety of grape has a specific yeast that will bring out its best qualities. Discuss with your supplier which is the best yeast for you to use.

Ideally, Australian white wine grapes are picked early in the morning in autumn, when the temperature is low (approximately 5°C), which is similar to traditional European temperatures. The coolness decreases the natural oxidation and fermentation that begins immediately once the grapes are picked, and which is particularly prevalent in white wine. Ensure your grapes are carried and stored in clean plastic containers to decrease bacterial contamination (avoid contact with reactive metals such as copper and iron, which cause excessive oxidation).

Use the grape-crushing machine (de-stemmer) to crush the grapes into the large, open plastic vat. Preferably do this while it is still cool outside, say 5–10°C.

De-stem and remove the stalks from the crushed grapes for best results (the newer grape-crushing machines will do this for you during the crushing process).

Measure how much grape juice you now have in the vat. If the grapes are good quality, add 10 g potassium metabisulfite per 100 litres of grape juice (if the grapes are a bit damaged or bruised, add 20 g per 100 litres). This will kill any wild yeast and prevent oxidation, which will taint the wine and turn it brown.

Press the crushed grapes immediately with the wine press, then transfer the juice to the first set of stainless-steel containers. Keep any excess pressed juice in the 10 litre plastic or stainless-steel containers (or demijohns), as you will need this to top up fermenting containers later.

Use the pH meter or litmus paper to check the pH, which should be 3.1–3.4. If it is above 3.4, add tartaric acid at a rate of 50 g per 0.1 pH above 3.4 (so if the pH is 3.6, add 100 g of tartaric acid per 100 litres of juice). Now test with the hydrometer. The reading should be at 12–14 baume. Add the sachet of Enzym Cultivar (a granulated pectinase for faster settling of whites) and mix. Seal the containers and leave for 12 hours.

Transfer the juice to the second set of stainless-steel containers and only fill to approximately three-quarters full – this allows the fermentation to continue and not spill over. Leave any sediment behind, as this will give the wine a cleaner flavour. Weigh 12.5 g of yeast nutrient (DAP) per 100 litres of juice. Dissolve in some juice and divide evenly among the containers, stirring in gently. Measure 25 g of a good-quality white wine yeast per 100 litres of grape juice and sprinkle on the surface of ten times its weight of warm (37°C) water. Leave for 15–20 minutes, then stir gently and divide evenly among the containers. Fit the airlocks and allow the fermentation process to commence, which will take approximately 2 weeks. The temperature of the room should be 18–20°C.

Fermentation is complete when bubbles have stopped forming and the baume reading is less than zero. If the wine is still sweet, it may be too cold. Re-check the pH, which should be between 3.2 and 3.4. If higher than 3.4, add tartaric acid at the same rate as opposite.

Once the fermentation is finished, add bentonite at a rate of 0.5 g per litre and mix thoroughly. This is a clearing agent.

After 2 weeks, sterilise your original set of stainless-steel fermenting containers. To the empty containers, add potassium metabisulfite at a rate of 10 g per 100 litres of wine, or divide 25 Campden tablets or one crushed Tannisol tablet evenly among the containers. Rack the wine back into the original stainless-steel containers, without disturbing the sediment, filling the barrels as much as possible to exclude all air. Rack again after 2 months, then bottle, seal with corks and stand upright for 2 weeks before drinking or cellaring.

This type of wine is best drunk the same year it is made to savour its fresh, fruity flavour. It is fantastic with any food you can think of.

SHIRAZ
2015

Wine troubleshooting

Microbiological spoilage

Yeast and bacteria are the cause of this type of spoilage and there are two main types. The first is acetic acid bacteria, which produces vinegar and needs oxygen to grow. This is prevented by avoiding oxygen contact with the wine. The second is a surface-growing yeast, a mycoderm, which grows in the presence of air and low sulphur dioxide levels. This tends to occur in partially filled containers. So, ensure you fill the containers to the recommended level, and avoid storing in contaminated/unclean barrels.

Non-microbiological spoilage

Reactive metals, such as copper and iron, should be avoided as they cause rapid oxidation. This leads to browning of the wine and the formation of acetaldehyde. Proteins cause a haze that can be removed with the clearing agent bentonite.

Stuck fermentation

This usually means that the room temperature is too low or the sulphur dioxide content is too high. Firstly, try and bring the room temperature to 18°C. If after two days this does not start the fermentation, rack the juice into another container. As you do this, allow the juice to splash – this will encourage the sulphur dioxide to come off. Wait for a day. If nothing happens, add another container of yeast. If it still does nothing after a further two days, give your local wine-making suppliers a call and see if they can help!

There are many variants that can affect the quality and consistency of your homemade wines.

Crushing
When making red wine, removing the stems decreases the tannin. If you fully crush the berries and leave the stems, it will produce a high tannin, high colour red wine.

Draining off
This is the draining off of the grape juice from the skins and stems, before the fermentation process has begun. Early draining produces lower tannins and colour.

Harvest time
Early harvest (less than 12 baume) will produce a lighter alcohol content, higher acid and a more herbaceous character. A late harvest will produce a higher berry flavour, more colour and tannin, and higher alcohol and body.

Maceration
The longer the maceration (fermentation on the skin, seeds and stems), the higher the tannin and colour complexity. More colour and flavour are extracted from the skins as the alcohol level increases during fermentation. Two or three weeks should be enough for full flavour. Longer than that will smooth out some tannins but small batches are at greater risk of oxidation, so best not to leave it too long.

Malolactic fermentation
After the wine has finished fermenting, a secondary fermentation (malolactic fermentation) can proceed. Commercially, this is produced by adding the relevant bacteria (*Oenococcus oenii*). Natural attempts to produce this are very hit and miss, and often lead to unwanted fermentations in the bottle. It can be stopped by adding approximately 8 g of potassium metabisulfite during the racking in the form of powder or Campden tablets, and it is preferable to abnormal fermentation.

Pressing
Free run off (no pressing) produces approximately 80 per cent of the volume. In hot fermentation, there are less tannin and complex fermentation compounds left in the pressings. Therefore, the pressings are separated and not blended. In cold fermentation, there is less tannin in the run off and therefore the pressings are blended.

Temperature
Hot fermentation: approximately 25–30°C for red wines. This produces maximum colour quality, more complex flavours and characters with less berry flavour and higher tannins. Lower fermentation temperature of 15–20°C produces maximum berry flavour, lower tannins and a lower fermentation complexity.

Other wines

Vinello

Vinello is a very light, low-alcohol wine that can be a pleasant variation. It can be made with red or white wine grapes. In order to produce a good vinello, it is very important for the pressings not to oxidise. This is prevented by immediately pressing the crushed grapes, placing the pressed stems and skins in a plastic or stainless-steel vat, adding half as much water as the total volume of juice extracted, and adding 12.5 g of sodium metabisulfite per 100 litres. Cover, leave for 2 days to soak, then press again. Add 162 g of sugar per litre of juice – this will produce a 9 per cent alcohol vinello. Allow to ferment, then rack as for white wine (see page 232). Drink within 1 year.

Sparkling wine

Spumante

If you produce a good-quality white wine that is stable and clear, you can easily turn it into sparkling wine! Add 18 g of sugar per litre of wine (this will produce 3.5 atmospheres of pressure). You now need to add suitable yeast (use champagne yeast). When I lived in Italy, my friend Federico, who lived in Impruneta in the Chianti area just south of Florence, would add natural yeast in the form of three barley seeds. This would create the secondary fermentation, but it was a little unpredictable. To bottle, use only the thick champagne bottles, as many a serious accident has been caused by lighter bottles exploding. I wonder whether this is an act of God, and therefore not covered by your life insurance?

Next, seal the bottles with hollow plastic stoppers and wire. Lay the bottles on their sides for approximately 1 week at 16–20°C, and after that at approximately 12°C. Leave the bottles on their sides for approximately 1 year, gently shaking each month to dislodge the sediment.

After 1 year, lift the bottles to lean at a 45-degree angle, with the neck down. Every few days, rotate a quarter circle. This will encourage the sediment to travel into the hollow of the stopper. In order to remove the sediment, you need to encapsulate it in ice.

Firstly, cool the bottles to 6°C. Create a freezing mixture by combining three parts crushed ice with one part rock salt. This will create a temperature of -20°C. Immerse the bottlenecks in the freezing mixture for approximately 20 minutes, which should be enough to freeze the stopper. Remove the stopper gently, removing the yeast that has stuck to the stopper with it. Quickly top up the bottle if necessary with extra white wine, then reseal with a stopper without a cavity and rewire. Allow to rest for 3 months before drinking.

Condiments

You can make many wonderful things with the by-products of winemaking! Here are a few popular traditional recipes.

Boiled must

Mosto cotto

Mosto is a syrup made from freshly crushed grape juice (must). It is best made with the sweetest grapes. This will produce a very sweet syrup with a delicate toasted vanilla flavour. It's great in sweets and on ice cream, or as a granita in summer. It is also popular as the basis for the famous *mostardo*.

Note: *Mostardo* means different things to different Italians. This is an example of why there can never be total harmony between the Northern Italians and the *meridionali* (southerners). In the south, *mostardo* comes from the word *mosto* (grape must) and refers to a jammy paste (a little like Turkish delight) made from sweet grape juice. This is used in cakes and is also fantastic with a good gutsy blue cheese (not a traditional accompaniment). In the north, the word means mustard and is used to describe fruit preserved in mustard oil or powder, which is often served with boiled meats (see page 241).

Aeolian Islands must

Mostardo delle Eolie

10 litres freshly crushed grape juice
2 quinces, sliced
3 dried figs
1 tablespoon carob powder
50 g grape vine ash (this must be totally burned until it is white)
1 lemon branch, with leaves attached, for stirring!
560 g plain flour
2.2 kg almonds, toasted
20 g ground cinnamon

Place the grape juice, quince, figs, carob and ash in a large stockpot and bring to the boil. Constantly stir using the lemon branch. When the volume reduces by one-quarter, remove from the heat and allow to settle for 24 hours. Filter the boiled must through a clean muslin bag and return to the stockpot to re-boil. Add the flour, almonds and cinnamon. Stir until a spoonful stays solid when placed on a cold plate (as when making jam).

Pour the *mostardo* approximately 1 cm thick onto greased and lined baking trays or flat plates. Allow to cool at room temperature overnight. You can eat the *mostardo* fresh. If you wish to dry the *mostardo* to keep it for longer, place it outside in the shade on a bed of lemon leaves. Place a net over the top to keep flies away. At midday, turn the slabs over; repeat this process for 10 days.

Store the dried *mostardo* in an airtight container in the fridge, where it will keep almost indefinitely.

Sicilian must

Mostardo Siciliano

10 litres freshly crushed grape juice
150 g hazelnuts
150 g almonds, crushed
2 tablespoons currants
1 teaspoon ground cloves
1 kg plain flour

Pour the grape juice into a large stockpot over low heat and slowly bring to the boil. A thick scum will form on top; remove this carefully with a slotted spoon and discard. Cook the juice until it reduces down to one-third of its original volume.

Remove from the heat and add the hazelnuts, almonds, currants and cloves. Place the pot back on a low heat and slowly add the flour, stirring constantly until the mixture has the consistency of polenta or porridge. Pour onto greased and lined baking trays, or roll into logs with baking paper and tie with string. Allow to cool and dry out slowly, either on a wire rack or in a very low oven (approximately 100°C) until dry to your taste. Store the dried *mostardo* in an airtight container in the fridge, where it will keep almost indefinitely.

Variation

Mrs Giolando's grape juice must
Mostardo della Signora Giolando

Pour freshly crushed grape juice into a large stockpot over low heat. Add approximately 100 g of corn flour (already mixed with a little juice) for every litre of juice, then bring slowly to the boil. A thick scum will form on top; remove this carefully with a slotted spoon and discard. Keep stirring until the *mosto* is a firm consistency and has reduced to approximately one-third of its original volume. Before pouring out onto a greased and lined baking tray, add 10 g of freshly toasted and coarsely crushed almonds, 10 g of raisins and 10 g of chopped dried figs for every litre of juice. The amount depends on your taste. Pour out onto the tray and allow to cool and set. You can then either leave it as is and eat it fresh or you can store it for later. If you are going to do this, place the tray in a very low oven (approximately 100°C) until dry to your taste. Cut the *mostardo* into small cubes and store in an airtight container in the fridge with a coating of caster sugar. It will keep almost indefinitely.

Cremona mustard

Mostarda di Cremona

This is a spicy, sweet mustard that is eaten with boiled or white meats. It has a sharp, sweet flavour. This recipe originated as a means of preserving fruit for the year.

100 g apricots, halved and stones removed
50 g oranges, peeled and halved
50 g figs (fresh or dried)
100 g firm green apples, peeled and halved, cores removed
100 g firm yellow peaches, halved and stones removed
100 g mandarins, peeled
100 g brown pears, peeled and halved, cores removed
100 g glacé cherries
50 g glacé orange peel
400 g sugar
10 drops of mustard oil or 40 g white mustard powder

Place the fruit in a large stockpot and cover with the sugar. Leave to stand, uncovered, for 24 hours (do not cover the pot with a lid at any time during the standing or cooking process).

The next day, add 250 ml of water to the stockpot, place over medium–high heat and bring to the boil. Simmer, uncovered, for 5 minutes. Allow to cool and stand for another 24 hours.

The next day, bring the mixture to boiling point again and simmer, uncovered, for 5 minutes. Add the mustard and stir well.

Following the instructions on page 21, transfer the mixture to a clean jar, leaving a 2 cm gap at the top. Seal the jar hermetically in a hot water bath for 20 minutes to ensure it is airtight.

The *mostarda* will keep for up to 6 months stored in a cool, dark place, but is ready to eat straight away. Once opened, store in the fridge for up to 6 months.

Vinegar

Aceto

All the recipes in this book that require vinegar will be even better if made with homemade wine vinegar! This is the final process of winemaking. Like all products, the better the ingredients, the better the outcome. So, use a reasonable wine to start with. It is essential that there is no sulphur in the wine at all.

The essentials of vinegar are:

* red or white wine (without sulphur preservative)
* water (at a rate of two parts wine to one part water)
* oxygen, or air (you do not use an air lock for this process)
* the 'mother of vinegar', a bacterial starter that can be bought at a wine supply store, or one can be created by adding 4–5 strands of spaghetti to the barrel of wine/water mix. It will look like a layer of gelatinous slime that will float on top of the barrel.

The vinegar will take 3–4 months to be ready, at which point you can siphon it into clean bottles or jars (see steps 1–2, page 21). The vinegar can now be topped up as needed almost indefinitely. As you add more wine to the vinegar jar, always add two parts wine to one part vinegar.

Holy wine

Vin santo

Tuscany is famous for its chianti wine, which is available worldwide. Chianti is usually made from a blend of grapes, which tend to be planted in a haphazard mix, with each vineyard using a slightly different combination.

One year, we were lucky enough to help with the grape picking at Impruneta in Tuscany. My wife and children, along with other friends and helpers, picked grapes in the beautiful rolling hills of Tuscany, with the cypress trees punctuating the horizon. At lunch, we sat outdoors under a pergola and ate *panzarotta* (a local salad) with a bowl of *peposa delle fornaci* (fresh pecorino) and a cold tripe salad that is typical of the region. All of this was consumed with a glass of the last vintage and some of the typical unsalted Tuscan bread.

A dessert wine that the locals produce is *vin santo*, made from partially dried grapes of the region – a mix of mavasia, sangiovese and trebbiano grapes. The reason it is called *vin santo*, or holy wine, is because the grapes are crushed, pressed and placed in small oak barrels on Good Friday in Italy (Australia has similar weather in July).

To make 30 litres of *vin santo*, you will need 100 kg of grapes, small oak barrels and a cool, low-draught area. The grapes are picked late, when the sugar content is high, and hung to slowly partially dry. The barrels are only filled to two-thirds full and then sealed. The one-third air lock gives the fermenting juice some space to produce gas without exploding the barrels. It also allows a slow oxidation that produces the taste typical of this wine. The barrels are left resting, undisturbed, for 3 years. Then the wine is racked and bottled.

Traditionally, this is drunk with a *cantuccino*, a toasted almond biscuit typical of Florence.

Pickled turnips

Brevada di rape

When you make your own wine (see pages 228–233), always keep the grape pressings and allow them to turn into vinegar. Just leave the pressings in open crates and the vinegar fly will do this for you – it always seems to know when it is *vendemmia* (grape harvest) time. The grape pressings can then be used to pickle vegetables, as below.

whole turnips, trimmed and peeled
grape pressings from wine making
    (see pages 230–233)
extra-virgin olive oil
salt, to taste

Bury the turnips in the vinegary grape pressings, which should be stored in a wooden, plastic or stainless-steel container. Leave in a cool place for 2 months, by which time the turnips will be pickled with the vinegar. Rinse the grape pressings off, place the turnips in vacuum-sealed bags and freeze. When you want to eat the turnips, grate them coarsely. Cook in olive oil over very low heat for 2–3 hours, adding a splash of water as needed and salt to taste. This pickled turnip is delicious served with *Cotechino* (see page 211).

Variation

Pickled cabbage
Conserve di cavolo cappuccio

Follow the recipe above but use a quartered cabbage instead. Leave the cabbage, completely covered in the grape pressings, for 1 month, perhaps 6 weeks. When you want to eat the cabbage, remove it from the pressings, shred finely and cook as above. This pickled cabbage is delicious served with *Cotechino* (see page 21).

'In 1992, we had some visitors from Ischia whom we had met the previous year in Bali! Daniela, Assunta and Elio came with many gifts, one of which was a bottle of *limoncino* made by Assunta's mother. It was magnificent.

The following year, we spent a perfect week with them in Ischia, in the Bay of Naples, overwhelmed by their hospitality and generosity. Each day was filled with fairytale experiences for our children and ourselves. We sampled (or rather gorged on) the most authentic *cucina Napolitana casalinga* (Neapolitan home cooking).

One day, we were taken to a restaurant called La Sgarrubbata. We left the marina of Sant'Angelo in a flotilla of small boats into the turquoise crystal-clear waters, stopping to dive for sea urchins, which we ate fresh with a squeeze of lemon. After 20 minutes of rugged coastline, we arrived at a small bay and were told that the only way to the restaurant was to swim to shore. Only one problem: I cannot swim. So, they threw me overboard with a life vest and towed me to shore! Awaiting us was a long wooden table filled with freshly cut yellow peaches and jugs of chilled local wine.

The meal began with marinated sardines and tuna, a variety of sun-dried tomatoes *sott'olio*, freshly cut local prosciutto and crusty bread. Then came *pasta marinara* – an alchemic blend of fresh tomatoes, golden olive oil, incredibly fresh local shellfish, garlic and pasta cooked to perfection. There was also a *pasta all'arrabiata,* a simple, fiery pasta made with fresh local tomatoes that cemented my appreciation for simplicity.

Then followed free-range chicken and swordfish on coals and a variety of vegetables cooked simply with local olive oil. Next came rabbit cooked with sage and white wine, simmered for three hours. Throughout the meal we were brought carafes of crisp white wine and bottles of homemade *limoncino*. Finally, we had a blissful, post-lunch nap stretched out on lilos on a balcony in the sun. Such generous, vibrant hospitality. It was a long time ago but as you can tell, I have never forgotten it. That is Italy. When you have a good food experience there, you will remember it forever.'

Liqueurs

As far back as I can remember, I recall our family visiting friends or *compari*, always with something from the garden, a string of sausages, a bottle of liqueur, marsala or wine. We would never visit without an exchange of gifts, often returning home with more than we had brought.

There are no bottle shops in Varapodio, as in most Italian villages, and it took a while for it to occur to me that of course people hadn't bought the liqueurs or wine – they had made it themselves!

In Italy, people have been making traditional alcoholic drinks at home for thousands of years. Here in Australia, it is a bit different – while you can make beer or wine at home, no problem, it is in fact illegal to make your own spirits or liqueurs, even for personal use, without a licence. All the recipes that follow use pure alcohol and therefore if you're making them at home in Australia, you need to ensure you're doing it legally.

Assuming you have all the right approvals in place, you can buy the 60 per cent proof alcohol needed for these recipes from specialist suppliers. All the following liqueurs are best kept in the freezer, to be served ice cold.

Limoncino liqueur from Capri

Limoncino di Capri

This recipe produces a liqueur that, as a friend once stated, 'warms places in my body that I did not even know I had'.

peel of 10 lemons (make sure to remove the bitter white pith)
1 litre 60% proof alcohol
270 g sugar

Place the lemon peel in a jar and pour over the alcohol, then seal and leave to stand for 10 days. If you allow the skins to remain in the alcohol too long, the final *limoncino* will be cloudy rather than golden and clear. Strain the lemon-infused alcohol into a container, then add the sugar and 670 ml of water. Cover and allow to stand for approximately 1 month, then siphon into a clean bottle (see steps 1–2, page 21) and store in a cool, dark place for up to 1 year.

Before you drink the *limoncino*, place the bottle in the freezer and serve ice cold. This allows the alcohol to be a little disguised, erupting like Vesuvius inside your stomach.

Variation

Cream of limoncello

Use the peel of only 4 lemons (make sure to remove the bitter white pith), plus 1 litre 60 per cent proof alcohol, 1.3 kg sugar, 1.3 litres milk and 2 teaspoons vanilla essence.

Infuse the lemon peel in the alcohol for 5 days, then strain the lemon-infused alcohol into a container and set aside. Heat the milk and sugar and bring to the boil for 2–3 minutes. Strain the milk mixture into a container and allow to cool. Repeat this process twice more. After the third time it has cooled, add the vanilla essence, strain and mix with the lemon-infused alcohol. Siphon into a clean bottle (see steps 1–2, page 21) and stand for 1 week, then serve ice cold from the freezer.

Other variations include Antonio's 'secret' (not anymore, now everyone will know it) of adding 2–3 lemon leaves and the peel of 1 lime to the alcohol infusion. This will produce a much tangier taste. You could also use any other citrus peel – the peels of 6–8 oranges will produce a Grand Marnier–like liqueur, for example.

Basil liqueur

Basilichino

100 basil leaves
1 litre 60% proof alcohol
270 g sugar

Place the basil leaves in a jar and pour over the alcohol, then seal and allow to stand for 10 days. Strain the basil-infused alcohol into a container, then add the sugar and 670 ml of water. Cover and allow to stand for 1 month, then siphon into a clean bottle (see steps 1–2, page 21) and store in a cool, dark place for up to 1 year. Serve ice cold from the freezer.

Abruzzi walnut liqueur

Nocino degli Abruzzi

28 green walnuts, halved
10 cloves
peel of 1 lemon
1 litre 60% proof alcohol
330 g sugar

Place the halved walnuts, cloves and lemon peel in a jar and pour over the alcohol, then seal and allow to stand for 40 days. Strain the infused alcohol into a container, then add the sugar and 670 ml of water. Cover and allow to stand for 1 month, then siphon into a clean bottle (see steps 1–2, page 21) and store in a cool, dark place for up to 1 year. Serve ice cold from the freezer.

Loquat liqueur

Nespolino

This recipe uses the pips of the *nespoli* or loquat. The resulting liqueur is like a nutty amaretto.

80 loquat pips (do not peel)
1 litre 60% proof alcohol
270 g sugar

Place the loquat pips in a jar and pour over the alcohol, then seal and allow to stand for 30 days. Strain the infused alcohol into a container, then add the sugar and 670 ml of water. Cover and allow to stand for 1 month, then siphon into a clean bottle (see steps 1–2, page 21) and store in a cool, dark place for up to 1 year. Serve ice cold from the freezer.

Walnut liqueur

Nocino

It is interesting how religion plays a part in the pleasures of the Italian. In Italy, green walnuts are picked on June 24 (the feast of St John); in Australia this is equivalent to late December. They are then allowed to stand for 40 days, like the 40 days of Lent.

24 green walnuts, quartered
10 cloves
1 whole nutmeg
1 cinnamon stick
1 litre 60% proof alcohol
165 g sugar

Place the walnuts and spices in a jar and pour over the alcohol, then seal and allow to stand for 40 days. Strain the infused alcohol into a clean bottle (see steps 1–2, page 21), then add the sugar and 200 ml of water. Seal and allow to stand for 1 month, then store in a cool, dark place for up to 1 year. Serve ice cold from the freezer.

Neapolitan walnut liqueur

Nocino di Napoli

20 green walnuts, quartered
2–3 cloves
peel of ½ lemon
small handful of perfumed rose petals
750 ml 60% proof alcohol
230 g sugar

Place the walnuts, cloves, lemon peel and rose petals in a jar and pour over the alcohol, then seal and allow to stand for 40 days. Dissolve the sugar in 130 ml of water. Strain the infused alcohol into a clean bottle (see steps 1–2, page 21), then add the sugar syrup. Store in a cool, dark place for 1 week before drinking. It will keep for up to 1 year unopened. Serve ice cold from the freezer.

Rose liqueur

Rosolio

200 g perfumed rose petals, roughly crushed using a mortar and pestle
700 ml 60% proof alcohol
530 g sugar

Place the crushed rose petals in a jar and pour over the alcohol, then seal and allow to stand for 10 days. Dissolve the sugar in 400 ml of water, then add to the alcohol infusion and leave to stand for a further 40 days. Strain the alcohol infusion into a clean bottle (see steps 1–2, page 21), then store in a cool, dark place for up to 1 year. Serve ice cold from the freezer.

Aniseed liqueur

Anice

40 g star anise
2 g coriander seeds
3 cloves
1 cinnamon stick
1 vanilla pod
peel of ½ orange
400 ml 60% proof alcohol
235 g sugar

Combine the spices and orange peel in a jar and pour over the alcohol, then seal and allow to stand for 20 days. Dissolve the sugar in 270 ml of water. Strain the infused alcohol into a clean bottle (see steps 1–2, page 21), then add the sugar syrup. Allow to stand for 1 month, then store in a cool, dark place for up to 1 year. Serve ice cold from the freezer.

Bay leaf liqueur

Laurino

500 g fresh bay leaves
500 ml 60% proof alcohol
300 g sugar

Place the bay leaves in a jar and pour over the alcohol, then seal and allow to stand for 45 days. Strain the alcohol infusion into a clean bottle (see steps 1–2, page 21). Dissolve the sugar in 330 ml of water, then add to the alcohol infusion and leave to stand for 1 month. Store in a cool, dark place for up to 1 year. Serve ice cold from the freezer.

Orange liqueur

Liquore d'arancia

peel of 500 g oranges (white pith removed),
    sliced into thin strips
300 g sugar
350 ml 60% proof alcohol

Place the orange peel in a jar with the sugar,
alcohol and 270 ml of water. Seal and allow
to stand for 15 days. Strain into a clean bottle
(see steps 1–2, page 21) and store in a cool,
dark place for up to 1 year. Serve ice cold
from the freezer.

Raspberry liqueur

Liquore di lamponi

150 g fresh raspberries
1 litre 40% proof alcohol
50 ml ready-made sugar syrup

Place the raspberries and alcohol in a jar,
seal and leave to stand for 2 months. Strain
(optional; the raspberries are nice to serve
with the liqueur) the alcohol infusion into
clean bottles or jars (see steps 1–2, page 21)
and add the sugar syrup, then leave to stand
for a further 2 months. Store in a cool, dark
place for up to 1 year. Serve ice cold from
the freezer.

Mandarin liqueur

Mandarinello

peel of 1 kg mandarins (white pith removed)
750 ml 60% proof alcohol
435 g sugar
230 ml hot water

Place the mandarin peel in a jar and
pour over the alcohol, then seal and allow
to stand for 10 days. Strain the alcohol infusion
into a clean bottle (see steps 1–2, page 21).
Dissolve the sugar in the hot water and
add to the alcohol infusion. Seal and store
in a cool, dark place for up to 1 year. Serve
ice cold from the freezer.

Mint liqueur

Liquore di menta

50 g mint leaves
600 ml 60% proof alcohol
200 g sugar

Place the mint leaves in a jar and pour over
the alcohol, then seal and allow to stand
for 8 days. Strain the alcohol infusion into
a clean bottle (see steps 1–2, page 21) –
a dark-coloured glass is best to ensure that
the colour of the liqueur remains a deep
green. Dissolve the sugar in 100 ml of water
and bring to the boil. Allow to cool, then add
to the alcohol. Leave to stand for 1 month,
then store in a cool, dark place for up to
1 year. Serve ice cold from the freezer.

Hundred herbs liqueur

Liqueur Centerbe

Centerbe is a famous liqueur from the small village of Tocco in Abruzzi.

1 cinnamon stick
2 cloves
3 fresh bay leaves
2 large basil leaves
3 dried chamomile flowers
2 sprigs crushed juniper berries
1 small marjoram sprig
1 small mint sprig
2 sage leaves
1 small rosemary sprig
3 leaves from a lemon tree
1 small thyme sprig
pinch of saffron
400 ml 60% proof alcohol
200 g sugar

Place the spices and herbs in a jar and cover with the alcohol, then seal and allow to stand for 1 month.

Dissolve the sugar in 200 ml of water and add to the infusion. Leave for 2 hours. Strain the alcohol infusion into a clean bottle or jar (see steps 1–2, page 21). Allow to stand for 3 months, then store in a cool, dark place for up to 1 year. Serve ice cold from the freezer.

Strawberry liqueur

Fragolino

1 kg strawberries, hulled
1 litre 60% proof alcohol
670 g sugar

Place the strawberries in a large jar and pour over the alcohol, then seal and allow to stand for 10 days.

Make a syrup with the sugar and 330 ml of water. Bring to simmering point, then allow to cool. Mix with the alcohol infusion, then leave to stand for another 20 days.

Strain the alcohol infusion into a clean bottle (see steps 1–2, page 21) and allow to stand for 1 month, then store in a cool, dark place for up to 1 year. Serve ice cold from the freezer.

Grappa

My *compare* Rennie, who comes from Pordenone in the Friuli, says that the Friulani make the best grappa. He tells me that when he arrived in Pordenone in late September, the air was heavy with a sweet scent of grappa. It literally enveloped the whole region like a dense fog. Each household had a still for brewing this *acqua santa* or holy water.

One can make grappa from the fermented grape pressings left over after making red wine (white wine doesn't work as the grape pressings aren't fermented). All you need is something with alcohol and the flavour of the wine. The best grapes for grappa are mataro, muscat and waltham cross. These tend to produce a more aromatic wine. They are sweeter grapes, leading to a higher yield.

The grapes are crushed in the normal way (see page 230) and allowed to ferment on the skin until fermentation has stopped. Make sure the barrel is covered to prevent vinegar fly tainting the must.

Set up the still – ensuring, if you are in Australia, you have the proper permits to do so. If you are distilling the grape pressings, firstly add a bucket of water to the pressings. This ensures there is liquid at the bottom of the still so that the skins will not burn or stick to the bottom. If you are using wine, just pour that into the still.

Only fill the still chamber to two-thirds of its capacity. If the chamber is too full, there is a chance that the skins may rise to the surface, or that the scum that forms on top of the wine will block the exhaust pipe. This could lead to increased pressure in the chamber, which can result in an explosion of overheated alcohol. I say 'can' – it does! One year, Dad decided that he did not have the time to boil multiple containers, and so he filled the chamber to the brim. The still began boiling but nothing was coming out, so he increased the flame. At that very moment, Mum called Dad out of the kitchen and luckily too – as he left, the still exploded! There was hot wine plastered all over the walls, and I was called in to clean the mess. I think we all learned from that day.

Seal the top of the still with fresh bread dough if it is loose fitting, or screw it down. Bring the contents of the still gradually to a temperature of 80°C. Do not heat it too quickly as you only want the alcohol to evaporate. This happens at 70°C. If the mixture boils, then water and other unwanted contaminants will also evaporate and the grappa will be weaker and of an inferior quality. As the alcohol evaporates, it will begin to slowly drip out of the end. Discard the first 10 per cent as this will be mostly pure alcohol. If it flows too quickly, there is probably too much heat under the container and too much water in the distillate. Collect the liquid in glass containers. Take a teaspoon of the distilled liquid and place a match to it (away from the still!). The grappa should ignite easily. If it does not, stop the distillation and discard the rest of the contents of the still.

To test the quality of the grappa, pour a little onto the palms of your hands and rub vigorously. The heat generated will evaporate the alcohol. The smell should be clean, slightly fragrant of the grapes, with no burnt or off aromas. The neat distillate can be diluted down with water to taste to drink, but if you are using it for preserving fruits and berries, leave it neat. Essentially, any fruit can be preserved in grappa (see overleaf for some ideas). The basic principle is to pickle the fruit or berries in the grappa and then to pickle yourself with it when you drink it!

Grappa variations

Aniseed grappa
Grappa all' anice

The process is the same as for grappa but with the addition of aniseed. Add approximately 2 kg of wild aniseed branches to a 50 litre container of fermentation.

Apricots in grappa
Albicocche in grappa (apré cosce)

Wash, halve and de-stone 2 kg of apricots. Arrange the halves in layers and sprinkle with 300 g of sugar. Cover with grappa. Seal and leave for 2 months before eating.

Blackberries in grappa
More in grappa

Layer 1.5 kg of blackberries in a jar with 750 g of sugar. Add 1 cinnamon stick, a few cloves and some lemon peel, then cover with grappa. Seal and leave for 1 month before eating.

Cherries in grappa
Ciliege in grappa

Take 1 kg of cherries, cut the stems short and place in a large jar. Dissolve 450 g of sugar in 125 ml of water, add to the cherries and cover with grappa. Add the peel of 1 lemon and seal. Leave for 3 months before eating.

Grapes in grappa
Uva in grappa

Wash 1 kg of sultana or muscat grapes. Place in a glass jar and add 1 vanilla pod, 1 cinnamon stick and the peel of 1 lemon, then cover with grappa. Seal and leave for 1 month before eating.

Grappa with mint
Grappa con la menta

The chocolate mint variety is fantastic for this recipe. Place 50 g, or a good handful, of mint leaves in a wide-necked, sealable jar. Cover with 1 litre of grappa. Leave for 20 days. Strain into a bottle and add 200 g of sugar. Mix and leave for 1 month before drinking.

Limoncino made with grappa
Limoncino fatto con grappa

Add the peels of 6 lemons (bitter white pith removed) to 1 litre of grappa. After 10 days, strain into a bottle and add 200 g of sugar. Leave to stand for another 2 weeks, then seal and drink ice cold from the freezer.

Oranges and coffee in grappa
Aranci e caffè in grappa

In a wide-necked 1 litre jar, place 25 coffee beans and 2 whole oranges, which you have pierced 10–15 times with a long needle. Cover with grappa and allow to stand 10 days. Strain the alcohol infusion into a bottle (reserve the coffee beans) and add 250 g of sugar. Allow to stand for 1 week. When serving, place a grappa-soaked coffee bean in the bottom of each glass.

Oranges in grappa
Aranci in grappa

Wash, cut and quarter (but don't peel) 1 kg of oranges. Place in layers with 250 g of sugar, 1 cinnamon stick and 2–3 cloves. Cover with grappa. Seal and leave for 1 month before eating.

Raspberries in grappa
Lamponi in grappa

Place 350 g of fresh raspberries, 1 litre of grappa, 1 cinnamon stick and 1–2 cloves in a jar, seal and leave in the sun for 40 days. Strain the alcohol infusion into a bottle. Leave for 1 month before drinking.

Redcurrants in grappa from Treviso
Ribes rosso in grappa di Treviso

Place 250 g of redcurrants in a jar with 1 litre of grappa. Leave for 20 days, then add 250 g of sugar. Allow to stand for 1 month, then bottle. Leave the redcurrants in the liqueur, as it is nice to serve the liqueur with some at the bottom of the glass.

Coffee zabaglione

Zabaglione al caffé

I make this for my wife every Sunday. This is not a preserve in the strictest sense of the word, except that it helps preserve every Italian marriage.

1 egg yolk
2 teaspoons sugar
1 tablespoon marsala
freshly brewed coffee

Place the egg yolk and sugar in a large mug and whisk until pale and thick. Add the marsala and keep stirring. Then, from a height, pour in freshly brewed coffee that has cooled very slightly (if the coffee is too hot, the egg yolk will curdle).

As you pour, stir up the froth and then serve. It is guaranteed to soothe any misunderstanding or upset.

Conversion charts

Measuring cups and spoons may vary slightly from one country to another, but the difference is generally not enough to affect a recipe. All cup and spoon measures are level.

One Australian metric measuring cup holds 250 ml (8 fl oz), one Australian metric tablespoon holds 20 ml (4 teaspoons) and one Australian metric teaspoon holds 5 ml. North America, New Zealand and the UK use a 15 ml (3-teaspoon) tablespoon.

Length

METRIC	IMPERIAL
3 mm	⅛ inch
6 mm	¼ inch
1 cm	½ inch
2.5 cm	1 inch
5 cm	2 inches
18 cm	7 inches
20 cm	8 inches
23 cm	9 inches
25 cm	10 inches
30 cm	12 inches

Liquid Measures

Pints

ONE AMERICAN PINT	ONE IMPERIAL PINT
500 ml (16 fl oz)	600 ml (20 fl oz)

Cups

CUP	METRIC	IMPERIAL
⅛ cup	30 ml	1 fl oz
¼ cup	60 ml	2 fl oz
⅓ cup	80 ml	2 ½ fl oz
½ cup	125 ml	4 fl oz
⅔ cup	160 ml	5 fl oz
¾ cup	180 ml	6 fl oz
1 cup	250 ml	8 fl oz
2 cups	500 ml	16 fl oz
2 ¼ cups	560 ml	20 fl oz
4 cups	1 litre	32 fl oz

Dry measures

The most accurate way to measure dry ingredients is to weigh them. However, if using a cup, add the ingredient loosely to the cup and level with a knife; don't compact the ingredient unless the recipe requests 'firmly packed'.

METRIC	IMPERIAL
15 g	½ oz
30 g	1 oz
60 g	2 oz
125 g	4 oz (¼ lb)
185 g	6 oz
250 g	8 oz (½ lb)
375 g	12 oz (¾ lb)
500 g	16 oz (1 lb)
1 kg	32 oz (2 lb)

Oven temperatures

Celsius to Fahrenheit

CELSIUS	FAHRENHEIT
100°C	200°F
120°C	250°F
150°C	300°F
160°C	325°F
180°C	350°F
200°C	400°F
220°C	425°F

Celsius to Gas Marks

CELSIUS	GAS MARK
100°C	200°F
120°C	250°F
150°C	300°F
160°C	325°F
180°C	350°F
200°C	400°F
220°C	425°F
110°C	¼
130°C	½
140°C	1
150°C	2
170°C	3
180°C	4
190°C	5
200°C	6
220°C	7
230°C	8
240°C	9
250°C	10

Thanks

How does one acknowledge the various contributions to this book?

I can never show enough admiration and thanks to my parents for their total commitment to history, culture, family and friends. For having sacrificed all that they had to give me, my brothers and sisters, and my children a much better opportunity for happiness.

Thanks to my wife, Lynn, and sons, Giuseppe, Carlo and Alessandro, for encouraging me, eating my food and valuing what I have to offer, and for understanding the importance of my background and putting up with my funny ways.

Thanks to the literally hundreds of *compare*, *commare*, friends and acquaintances who have shared their personal memories and stories with me.

Thanks to everyone who worked on this book: publisher Mary Small, project editor Clare Marshall, editor Philippa Moore, photographer Chris Middleton, stylist Deb Kaloper and the design and illustration team at Evi-O.Studio.

Thanks to you, the readers. I hope that by reading this book you can also reach into your past, your origins, and it will allow you all to share and celebrate the mixture of family, food, fun and friendship that is the basis of who we are and what we are.

Bocca al lupo and stay safe.

Index

R

raisins
- Beccucci's black pudding 218
- Mrs Giolando's grape juice must 240

raspberries
- Perfumed syrup 126
- Raspberries in grappa 256
- Raspberry liqueur 250
- Raspberry syrup 124

Raspberries in grappa 256
Raspberry liqueur 250
Raspberry syrup 124

redcurrants
- Perfumed syrup 126
- Redcurrants in grappa 256
- Redcurrant syrup 126

Redcurrant syrup 126
Redcurrants in grappa 256
Red wine 230–1
Ricotta 170
Ricotta from pecorino whey 177
Ricotta made from fresh pasteurised milk 171
Ricotta made from fresh pasteurised milk with fig branch 171
Ricotta made from fresh pasteurised milk with lemon 171
Ripe Calabrese olives, Greek style 92
Rivestita 193
Rosa's fried eggplant preserve 33
Rose liqueur 249
Rosemary's black olives 90
Rosetta's pickled vegetables 54

S

salami
- Abruzzese salami 193
- Armando's salami with fennel 194
- Calabrese salami 189
- Capocollo 199
- Cesare's capocollo 199
- Cesare's Italian salami 194
- Compare Peppino's capocollo 199
- Compare Vittorio's capocollo 199
- Dino Bertolin's prize-winning capocollo 199
- Fennel salami from Marco of San Giovanni Valdarno 196
- pressing into bungs 190–1
- Finocchiona di Beccucci 196
- hanging and curing 191–2
- making at home 186–92
- Mario's Tuscan salami 194
- Offal salami 208
- Rivestita 193
- Signora Fiorentino's liver salami from Molise 197
- Small salamis for sugo 197
- storing 192
- Stuffed hock salami from Emilia 198
- Stuffed pork bladder 198
- Tongue salami 211
- Tuscan capocollo 199
- Tuscan salami 194
- Venetian salami 193
- Ventricina spread 198
- *see also* sausages

Salt-cured beef 212
Salt-cured tuna 161
salt, preserving in 19
Salted anchovies 153
Salted basil 103
Salted capers 110
Salted fish roe 161
Salted herbs 103
Salted pork cheek 201
Salted ricotta 170
Salted topside 213

sardines
- Marinated sardines 153
- Marinated sardines in lemon juice 153
- Salted anchovies 153
- Sardines in oil 154
- Sardines in salt 152
- Sardines in saor 155

Sardines in oil 154
Sardines in salt 152
Sardines in saor 155

sauces
- Tomato sauce 120–1
- *see also* pestos

sausages
- Cotechino 211
- Cotechino from Bologna 211
- Dino's fresh sausages 208
- Enzo and Tina's liver sausages 209
- Fresh sausages from Lucca 208
- Liver sausages 209
- Maria Luisa and Gabriella's terrine sausage from Le Marche 210
- Oreste's fresh sausages 208
- pressing into bungs 190–1
- Signora Fiorentino's soppressate from Molise 211
- storing 192
- *see also* black pudding, salami

Scottish thistles 43
seafood *see* calamari, octopus, mussels, pipis, prawns, squid
Sicilian must 240

A Plum book

This edition published in 2021 by
Pan Macmillan Australia Pty Limited
Level 25, 1 Market Street,
Sydney, NSW 2000, Australia

Level 3, 112 Wellington Parade,
East Melbourne, VIC 3002, Australia

First published in 2008 by Pietro Demaio

Design and illustration by Evi-O.Studio | Evi O.,
    Nicole Ho and Kait Polkinghorne
Edited by Philippa Moore
Index by Helena Holmgren
Photography by Chris Middleton
Food and prop styling by Deborah Kaloper
Food preparation by Pietro Demaio
Typeset by Evi-O.Studio
Colour reproduction by Splitting Image Colour Studio
Printed and bound in China by 1010 Printing
    International Limited

The traditional recipes in this book have been collected
from families in Australia and Italy in an attempt to
preserve them for future generations. The author has
tried to keep the recipes as close to their original form
as possible, as an act of cultural preservation. While
every attempt has been made to verify ingredients and
instructions and update them for a current audience,
many of the recipes have never been documented
before and have been passed on by word of mouth,
sometimes over hundreds of years. Please let your
own taste and judgement be your guide – or ask your
compare or *commare* for advice! – and enjoy being
part of this ongoing tradition.

10 9 8 7 6 5 4